Presented to:

_____

From:

_____

Date:

_____

Jesus Calling®

FAMILY DEVOTIONAL

100 DEVOTIONS FOR FAMILIES TO ENJOY PEACE IN HIS PRESENCE

Sarah Young

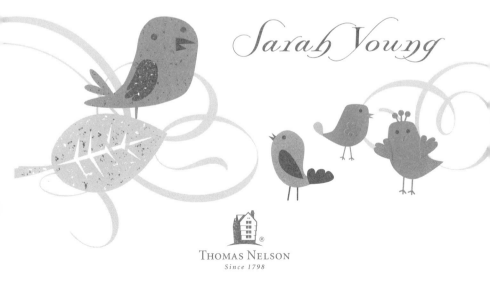

THOMAS NELSON
Since 1798

Published in Nashville, Tennessee, by Thomas Nelson. Thomas Nelson is a registered trademark of HarperCollins Christian Publishing, Inc.

Unless otherwise noted, Scripture quotations are taken from the Holy Bible, New International Version®, NIV®. Copyright © 1973, 1978, 1984 by Biblica, Inc.® Used by permission of Zondervan. All rights reserved worldwide. www.zondervan.com. The "NIV" and "New International Version" are trademarks registered in the United States Patent and Trademark Office by Biblica, Inc.®

Scripture quotations marked AMP are from the Amplified® Bible. Copyright © 1954, 1958, 1962, 1964, 1965, 1987 by The Lockman Foundation. Used by permission. (www.Lockman.org)

Scripture quotations marked ICB are taken from the International Children's Bible®. Copyright © 1986, 1988, 1999, 2015 by Thomas Nelson. Used by permission. All rights reserved.

Scripture quotations marked KJV are from the King James Version. Public domain.

Scripture quotations marked NASB are from New American Standard Bible®. Copyright © 1960, 1962, 1963, 1968, 1971, 1972, 1973, 1975, 1977, 1995 by The Lockman Foundation. Used by permission. (www.Lockman.org)

Scripture quotations marked NKJV are from the New King James Version®. © 1982 by Thomas Nelson. Used by permission. All rights reserved.

Any Internet addresses, phone numbers, or company or product information printed in this book are offered as a resource and are not intended in any way to be or to imply an endorsement by Thomas Nelson, nor does Thomas Nelson vouch for the existence, content, or services of these sites, phone numbers, companies, or products beyond the life of this book.

ISBN 978-1-4002-0995-8

The Library of Congress has cataloged the earlier edition as follows:

Young, Sarah, 1946–
Jesus Calling / by Sarah Young.
p. cm.
ISBN 978-1-59145-188-4 (hardcover)
1. Devotional calendars. 2. Devotional literature, English. I. Title.
BV4811.Y675 2004
242'.2—dc22   2044005474

Printed in Malaysia

23 24 25 26 27 OFF 6 5 4 3 2

INTRODUCTION

Dear Families,

You can get to know Jesus by praying and reading your Bible. It's important to understand how much Jesus loves you—and to enjoy Him as the Friend who is always with you.

The devotions in this book are written as if Jesus is speaking right to you. So "I," "Me," "My," and "Mine" are always about Jesus. I wrote the devotions this way to help you know that Jesus is with you all the time. He knows everything about you, and He loves you more than you can imagine!

Each entry in *Jesus Calling® Family Devotional* includes an adult devotion from *Jesus Calling®* and a corresponding children's devotion from *Jesus Calling®: 365 Devotions for Kids*. Parents and children can read their devotions separately or together and then come together to read Scripture aloud to dig deeper into the day's entries. The Bible is the only perfect Word of God, and each entry includes multiple Scripture verses. The "Talk Together" sections are questions designed to draw you closer to the Savior who is always with you as you spend time together in His presence.

Jesus loves you so much that He died on the cross to take the punishment for your sins. If you have never asked Him to be your Savior—forgiving all your sins—I hope you will do that very soon. It's the most important decision you will ever make! All the promises of the Bible are for you when Jesus is your Savior.

I hope you will find a quiet place and read these devotions slowly each day. Remember, Jesus is Immanuel—God with us. So He is God with you. I pray that you will enjoy His Presence and His Peace as you spend this time with Him.

BOUNTIFUL BLESSINGS,

Sarah Young

You will seek Me and find Me when you
search for Me with all your heart.

—Jeremiah 29:13 NASB

A RENEWED MIND

I AM RENEWING YOUR MIND. When your thoughts flow freely, they tend to move toward problems. Your focus gets snagged on a given problem, circling round and round it in attempts to gain mastery. Your energy is drained away from other matters through this negative focus. Worst of all, you lose sight of Me.

A renewed mind is Presence-focused. Train your mind to seek Me in every moment, every situation. Sometimes you can find Me in your surroundings: a lilting birdsong, a loved one's smile, golden sunlight. At other times, you must draw inward to find Me. I am always present in your spirit. Seek My Face, speak to Me, and I will light up your mind.

READ TOGETHER

Do not conform any longer to the pattern of this world, but be transformed by the renewing of your mind. Then you will be able to test and approve what God's will is—his good, pleasing and perfect will.

—ROMANS 12:2

READ MORE: HEBREWS 3:1; PSALM 105:4

A New Way of Thinking

I want to give you a new way of thinking. When you just let your thoughts wander, they tend to wander to your problems. Your mind swirls around and around, trying to solve them. You waste time and energy. Worst of all, your mind is so filled with your problems that you lose sight of Me.

Train your mind to look for Me wherever you are. I want your thoughts to be so filled with Me that you lose sight of your problems. I am all around you. Do you see Me? That bird singing, that smile from a friend, that ray of sunshine peeking through the clouds? I send each one your way. That feeling of safety and peace? That's from Me too. I'm always thinking about you. So think about Me.

TALK TOGETHER

Do your thoughts ever get stuck on your troubles? How can you "train your mind" to think about Jesus instead of those problems? What can you think about instead of your troubles?

A Thankful Attitude

A THANKFUL ATTITUDE opens windows of heaven. Spiritual blessings fall freely onto you through those openings into eternity. Moreover, as you look up with a grateful heart, you get glimpses of Glory through those windows. You cannot yet live in heaven, but you can experience foretastes of your ultimate home. Such samples of heavenly fare revive your hope. Thankfulness opens you up to these experiences, which then provide further reasons to be grateful. Thus your path becomes an upward spiral: ever increasing in gladness.

Thankfulness is not some sort of magic formula; it is the language of Love, which enables you to communicate intimately with Me. A thankful mind-set does not entail a denial of reality with its plethora of problems. Instead, it *rejoices in Me, your Savior,* in the midst of trials and tribulations. *I am your refuge and strength, an ever-present and well-proved help in trouble.*

READ TOGETHER

Though the fig tree does not bud and there are no grapes on the vines, though the olive crop fails and the fields produce no food, though there are no sheep in the pen and no cattle in the stalls, yet I will rejoice in the LORD, I will be joyful in God my Savior.

—HABAKKUK 3:17–18

READ MORE: EPHESIANS 1:3; PSALM 46:1 AMP

Windows of Heaven

When you come to Me with a thankful heart, it opens up windows of heaven. Spiritual blessings fall freely through those windows and down into your life. A thankful heart opens you up to these blessings, and then you have even *more* reasons to be grateful.

Being thankful brings you many blessings, but it is not a magic formula. Thankful words are really just the language of Love, and they help you grow closer to Me. When you thank Me, it makes a love-connection between your heart and Mine. Just as a telephone connection lets you talk to another person, a loving, thankful heart helps you talk to Me—and Me to you.

Being thankful doesn't mean you close your eyes to the many problems in this world. It means you find Joy in Me—your Savior—in the midst of a messed-up world. I am your hiding place and your strength. And I'm always ready to help you!

TALK TOGETHER

Can you name five things you're thankful for? Can you name ten? Can you name twenty? Why do you think being thankful makes you feel closer to God?

Rest in My Presence

Rest in My Presence when you need refreshment. Resting is not necessarily idleness, as people often perceive it. When you relax in My company, you are demonstrating trust in Me. *Trust* is a rich word, laden with meaning and direction for your life. I want you to *lean on, trust, and be confident in Me.* When you lean on Me for support, I delight in your trusting confidence.

Many people turn away from Me when they are exhausted. They associate Me with duty and diligence, so they try to hide from My Presence when they need a break from work. How this saddens Me! As I spoke through My prophet Isaiah: *In returning to Me and resting in Me you shall be saved; in quietness and trust shall be your strength.*

READ TOGETHER

For thus said the Lord God, the Holy One of Israel: In returning [to Me] and resting [in Me] you shall be saved; in quietness and in [trusting] confidence shall be your strength. But you would not.

—Isaiah 30:15 AMP

READ MORE: Psalm 91:1; Proverbs 3:5 AMP

Plug into Me!

Come to Me when you are tired and exhausted. Come to Me when you just need a break. Rest in My Presence. *Rest* is one of My gifts to you. It is not just being still. And it is *not* being lazy. Resting in Me shows that you trust Me enough to relax and lean on Me.

Some people actually run away from Me when they're tired. They think spending time with Me means more work, more responsibilities. So they hide from Me. But the truth is that I am the only place they can truly be recharged. It's a lot like plugging in your cell phone or your video game when the battery is low. Your phone or game waits quietly and then, after a while, it is ready to be used again. When you are tired and your battery is running low, plug into Me by resting in My Presence—and I will give you new strength.

TALK TOGETHER

How do you know when your "battery" is running low? What do you do to recharge? Have you tried resting in Jesus? What is the difference between sleeping and resting in Jesus?

SUFFERING FOR ME

BE PREPARED TO SUFFER FOR ME, in My Name. All suffering has meaning in My kingdom. Pain and problems are opportunities to demonstrate your trust in Me. Bearing your circumstances bravely—even thanking Me for them—is one of the highest forms of praise. This sacrifice of thanksgiving rings golden-toned bells of Joy throughout heavenly realms. On earth also, your patient suffering sends out ripples of good tidings in ever-widening circles.

When suffering strikes, remember that I am sovereign and that I can bring good out of everything. Do not try to run from pain or hide from problems. Instead, accept adversity in My Name, offering it up to Me for My purposes. Thus your suffering gains meaning and draws you closer to Me. Joy emerges from the ashes of adversity through your trust and thankfulness.

READ TOGETHER

Consider it pure joy, my brothers, whenever you face trials of many kinds, because you know that the testing of your faith develops perseverance. Perseverance must finish its work so that you may be mature and complete, not lacking anything.

—JAMES 1:2–4

READ MORE: PSALM 107:21–22; PSALM 33:21

Tough It Out

"Tough it out." "Stay strong." "Endure." You hear these words a lot when people are talking about sports. But they don't sound so great when you're talking about your life. And yet, that is what you must do: Tough it out, stay strong, and endure.

It's just a fact. You are going to have troubles in this life. The devil is your enemy. So he is going to throw everything he has at you. Problems at school, home, and with friends. Fear, loneliness, and doubt. Expect these troubles, and stand strong. And when the evil one attacks, give thanks.

Yes, give thanks! Thank Me for being able to bring good out of everything. Praise Me for the chance to see My Power in your life. Worship Me—the God who always has a purpose, and who will not let the evil one snatch you away. And thank Me for the spiritual strength you gain by enduring your troubles bravely.

TALK TOGETHER

Does it seem odd to be thankful when things are going wrong? Think of a trouble you've had to go through. Do you know Jesus was with you through every step of that trouble?

Let My Light Envelop You

WHEN YOUR SINS WEIGH HEAVILY upon you, come to Me. Confess your wrongdoing, which I know all about before you say a word. Stay in the Light of My Presence, receiving forgiveness, cleansing, and healing. Remember that *I have clothed you in My righteousness*, so nothing can separate you from Me. Whenever you stumble or fall, I am there to help you up.

Man's tendency is to hide from his sin, seeking refuge in the darkness. There he indulges in self-pity, denial, self-righteousness, blaming, and hatred. But *I am the Light of the world*, and My illumination decimates the darkness. Come close to Me and let My Light envelop you, driving out darkness and permeating you with Peace.

READ TOGETHER

But if we walk in the light, as he is in the light, we have fellowship with one another, and the blood of Jesus, his Son, purifies us from all sin.

—1 JOHN 1:7

READ MORE: ISAIAH 61:10; JOHN 8:12

Live in My Light

When you carry around sins, it is like carrying a backpack filled with rocks. The rocks are called *shame*, *guilt*, *self-pity*, *jealousy*, and even *hatred*. As time goes on, your pack gets heavier and heavier, pulling you down.

Give it to Me, all of it. Tell me your sins and hand over that backpack. I want to dump out all the heavy rocks. Then I want to fill your backpack up again with *love*, *mercy*, *forgiveness*, *joy*, and *peace*. Instead of weighing you down, these things will lift you up and make your journey easier.

Don't be embarrassed to bring your sins to Me. I already know all about them, and I'm just waiting to forgive you. That is why I died on the cross—to take the punishment for your sins. Don't live in the darkness of sin. Live in the Light of My forgiveness.

TALK TOGETHER

If you think about sins like heavy rocks, what are some of the "rocks" you are carrying around? Why do those sins feel heavy? How can prayer help you get rid of them? What would you like Jesus to fill your backpack with instead?

DEPEND ON ME

LIVING IN DEPENDENCE ON ME is a glorious adventure. Most people scurry around busily, trying to accomplish things through their own strength and ability. Some succeed enormously; others fail miserably. But both groups miss what life is meant to be: living and working in collaboration with Me.

When you depend on Me continually, your whole perspective changes. You see miracles happening all around, while others see only natural occurrences and "coincidences." You begin each day with joyful expectation, watching to see what I will do. You accept weakness as a gift from Me, knowing that *My Power plugs in most readily to consecrated weakness.* You keep your plans tentative, knowing that My plans are far superior. *You consciously live, move, and have your being in Me*, desiring that I live in you. I in you and you in Me. This is the intimate adventure I offer you.

READ TOGETHER

"On that day you will realize that I am in my Father, and you are in me, and I am in you."

—JOHN 14:20

READ MORE: 2 CORINTHIANS 12:9–10;
ACTS 17:28; COLOSSIANS 2:6–7

An Adventure with Me

Living your life while depending on Me is a great adventure. Most people—grown-ups and kids alike—scurry around trying to do things their own way. Some are huge successes; others fail miserably. But both miss out on what life is supposed to be—*an adventure with Me.*

When you give control of your life to Me, I open your eyes so that you can see Me at work in the world. Where others see "coincidences," you see My wonderful work—even miracles at times. And where others see only an everyday happening, you see Me.

Live each day just watching for what I will do next. You are in Me, and I am in you—and through Me you learn to truly live. This is the amazing adventure I offer you.

TALK TOGETHER

For any great adventure, you need a guide. Are you letting Jesus guide you? How can you make sure He is your Guide through this adventure of your life?

PATHS OF PEACE

I AM THE *PRINCE OF PEACE*. As I said to My disciples, I say also to you: *Peace be with you.* Since I am your constant Companion, My Peace is steadfastly with you. When you keep your focus on Me, you experience both My Presence and My Peace. Worship Me as King of kings, Lord of lords, and Prince of Peace.

You need My Peace each moment to accomplish My purposes in your life. Sometimes you are tempted to take shortcuts in order to reach your goal as quickly as possible. But if the shortcut requires turning your back on My peaceful Presence, you must choose the longer route. Walk with Me along paths of Peace; enjoy the journey in My Presence.

READ TOGETHER

For to us a child is born, to us a son is given, and the government will be on his shoulders. And he will be called Wonderful Counselor, Mighty God, Everlasting Father, Prince of Peace.

—ISAIAH 9:6

READ MORE: JOHN 20:19–21; PSALM 25:4 NKJV

Prince of Peace

I have many names: Wonderful Counselor, Mighty God, Everlasting Father, Prince of Peace, King of kings and Lord of lords. But in this messed-up world, it is perhaps as Prince of Peace that you need Me most.

Because I never leave your side, My Peace is always with you. You need this Peace each moment to live out My plan for your life. Sometimes you may want to take shortcuts—to reach your goal as quickly as possible. But if taking the shortcut means you turn your back on My peaceful Presence, then don't do it. Keep walking with Me along paths of Peace—even in this crazy world.

TALK TOGETHER

Jesus has many names, and one of them is Prince of Peace. How does Jesus' Presence make you feel peaceful? How do you spend time with Jesus?

Trust in Me Always

Strive to trust Me in more and more areas of your life. Anything that tends to make you anxious is a growth opportunity. Instead of running away from these challenges, embrace them, eager to gain all the blessings I have hidden in the difficulties. If you believe that I am sovereign over every aspect of your life, it is possible to trust Me in all situations. Don't waste energy regretting the way things are or thinking about what might have been. Start at the present moment—accepting things exactly as they are—and search for My way in the midst of those circumstances.

Trust is like a staff you can lean on as you journey uphill with Me. If you are trusting in Me consistently, the staff will bear as much of your weight as needed. *Lean on, trust, and be confident in Me with all your heart and mind.*

READ TOGETHER

Lean on, trust in, and be confident in the Lord with all your heart and mind and do not rely on your own insight or understanding. In all your ways know, recognize, and acknowledge Him, and He will direct and make straight and plain your paths.

—Proverbs 3:5–6 AMP

Read More: Psalm 52:8

Hidden Blessings

Learn to trust Me in all situations—the tough ones, as well as the easy ones. Trust Me when you don't understand what's going on. Trust Me when everything seems to be spinning out of control. Trust Me when you feel like you are all alone and no one understands. *I understand.*

Don't waste your time thinking about how things should have been. Don't try to run away. Start right this minute—accepting things exactly as they are—and search for My way through your challenges. Learn to look for the blessings and the opportunities I have hidden in those difficulties. Trust Me and lean on Me. I love you, and I will never let you down.

TALK TOGETHER

Trust is a big thing. What does it mean to trust someone? What does it mean to trust Jesus? How does your life show that you trust Jesus?

POTTER AND CLAY

I AM THE POTTER; you are My clay. I designed you before the foundation of the world. I arrange the events of each day to form you into this preconceived pattern. My everlasting Love is at work in every event of your life. On some days your will and Mine flow smoothly together. You tend to feel in control of your life when our wills are in harmony. On other days you feel as if you are swimming upstream, against the current of My purposes. When that happens, stop and seek My Face. The opposition you feel may be from Me, or it may be from the evil one.

Talk with Me about what you are experiencing. Let My Spirit guide you through treacherous waters. As you move through the turbulent stream with Me, let circumstances mold you into the one I desire you to be. Say *yes* to your Potter as you go through this day.

READ TOGETHER

Yet, O LORD, you are our Father. We are the clay, you are the potter; we are all the work of your hand.

—ISAIAH 64:8

READ MORE: PSALM 27:8; 1 JOHN 5:5–6 NKJV

I Am the Potter

Have you ever watched a potter form a piece of art from a lump of clay? Before the potter even begins to shape the clay, he has a plan in mind. It will be a bowl, a vase, a pitcher. He knows exactly what he is going to make and how he is going to use the finished piece. Every detail is formed with love.

You are My clay, and I am your Potter. Before the world was made, I designed you. I have a plan for you in My kingdom. You will be an encourager, a good friend, a sharer of My Word. I shape every day, every event of your life, with Love.

As you go through your day, talk to Me. Let Me show you how this day—with all its joys and troubles—can shape you into the masterpiece I designed you to be.

TALK TOGETHER

Think about how a potter shapes the clay. Sometimes he smooths it gently, but sometimes he pushes and molds it into the shape he wants. How does Jesus mold and shape you?

I Am All Around You

I AM ALL AROUND YOU, hovering over you even as you seek My Face. I am nearer than you dare believe, closer than the air you breathe. If My children could only recognize My Presence, they would never feel lonely again. *I know every thought before you think it, every word before you speak it.* My Presence impinges on your innermost being. Can you see the absurdity of trying to hide anything from Me? You can easily deceive other people, and even yourself, but I read you like an open, large-print book.

Deep within themselves, most people have some awareness of My imminent Presence. Many people run from Me and vehemently deny My existence because My closeness terrifies them. But My own children have nothing to fear, for I have cleansed them by My blood and clothed them in My righteousness. Be blessed by My intimate nearness. Since I live in you, let Me also live through you, shining My Light into the darkness.

READ TOGETHER

O LORD, you have searched me and you know me. You know when I sit and when I rise; you perceive my thoughts from afar. You discern my going out and my lying down; you are familiar with all my ways. Before a word is on my tongue you know it completely, O LORD.

—PSALM 139:1–4

READ MORE: EPHESIANS 2:13; 2 CORINTHIANS 5:21

An Open Book

I am all around you. I am nearer than you dare to believe—closer even than the air you breathe. I know every thought before you think it, every word before you say it. So you can see how silly it is to try to hide anything from Me!

You may be able to fool your parents, your teachers, and your friends. But you can never fool Me. I can read you like an open book. I know every secret, every sin. But I don't say this to make you afraid, or to make you feel guilty or ashamed. I say this so that you will *never* feel unloved or lonely again.

Listen carefully as I say this: I know everything about you—and still I will *never* leave you, and I will *never* stop loving you. I have removed all your sins so that you can be this close to Me.

TALK TOGETHER

Jesus knows every single thing about you—the good, the bad, and everything in between—and He still loves you. He will never stop loving you. Do you really, really believe that Jesus loves you?

Thank Me for My Spirit

Thank Me for the glorious gift of My Spirit. This is like priming the pump of a well. As you bring Me the sacrifice of thanksgiving, regardless of your feelings, My Spirit is able to work more freely within you. This produces more thankfulness and more freedom, until you are overflowing with gratitude.

I shower blessings on you daily, but sometimes you don't perceive them. When your mind is stuck on a negative focus, you see neither Me nor My gifts. In faith, thank Me for whatever is preoccupying your mind. This will clear the blockage so that you can find Me.

READ TOGETHER

Now it is God who has made us for this very purpose and has given us the Spirit as a deposit, guaranteeing what is to come.

—2 Corinthians 5:5

Read More: Psalm 50:14;
2 Corinthians 3:17; Psalm 95:2 nkjv

The Gift of the Spirit

I shower blessings down on you every day. Even when you don't notice them, they are there.

One of my greatest blessings is the gift of the Holy Spirit. He lives within you, teaching and guiding you.

The Holy Spirit is like a great multiplier. In math, five plus five equals ten. But five *times* five equals twenty-five—a much bigger result. The Holy Spirit works in much the same way. He takes your faith and multiplies it. You may start with a small bit of faith in Me, but the Spirit works to multiply it so that it grows much greater.

Be sure to thank Me for the gift of My Spirit. This helps Him to work more freely in you, making you even *more* thankful—and more joyful too!

TALK TOGETHER

Every day is filled with showers of blessings. Why are those blessings sometimes hard to see? How does the Holy Spirit help you see your blessings?

No Fear

I want to be Central in your entire being. When your focus is firmly on Me, My Peace displaces fears and worries. They will encircle you, seeking entrance, so you must stay alert. Let trust and thankfulness stand guard, turning back fear before it can gain a foothold. *There is no fear in My Love*, which shines on you continually. Sit quietly in My Love-Light while I bless you with radiant Peace. Turn your whole being to trusting and loving Me.

READ TOGETHER

There is no fear in love. But perfect love drives out fear, because fear has to do with punishment. The one who fears is not made perfect in love.

—1 John 4:18

Read More: 2 Thessalonians 3:16;
Numbers 6:25–26 nkjv

When You Are Afraid . . .

I want to be the Center of your life. When you focus on Me, My Peace chases away your fears and worries.

I know . . . *everyone* is afraid sometimes. I am not saying that you will *never* be afraid. What I am saying is that you never have to face your fears alone. I am *always* with you, and My Strength is *always* there for you. I will *never* leave you.

But fear is a sneaky thing. Just when you think you've gotten it out of your life, it will creep up behind and whisper in your ear: *You're all alone.* But remember My words: *I am always with you.*

Thank Me for My Presence, and trust Me; this will protect you from fear. Spend time in the Light of My Love, while I bless you with My Peace.

TALK TOGETHER

Are there certain things that frighten you? How is God bigger than each of those fears? How does He protect you?

Listen to Me

Learn to listen to Me even while you are listening to other people. As they open their souls to your scrutiny, *you are on holy ground.* You need the help of My Spirit to respond appropriately. Ask Him to think through you, live through you, love through you. My own Being is alive within you in the Person of the Holy Spirit. If you respond to others' needs through your unaided thought processes, you offer them dry crumbs. When the Spirit empowers your listening and speaking, My *streams of living water flow* through you to other people. Be a channel of My Love, Joy, and Peace by listening to Me as you listen to others.

READ TOGETHER

"Whoever believes in me, as the Scripture has said, streams of living water will flow from within him." By this he meant the Spirit, whom those who believed in him were later to receive. Up to that time the Spirit had not been given, since Jesus had not yet been glorified.

—John 7:38–39

Read More: Exodus 3:5; 1 Corinthians 6:19

While You Listen

Learn to listen to Me even while you are listening to others. When a friend trusts you enough to pour out heart, soul, and troubles to you, you are standing on holy ground. And you have a holy opportunity to help. But if you use only your own thoughts and wisdom to help that person, then what you are offering is only dry crumbs.

Instead, call on the Holy Spirit living inside you. Ask Him to think through you, live through you, love through you. Ask Him for the words to say.

The Spirit fills you with streams of living water—My Love, Joy, and Peace. When you let Him control your listening and speaking, that living water flows through you to others. So listen to Me while you're listening to others. You'll be a blessing to them—and you will be blessed too.

TALK TOGETHER

Are you a good friend? Do others tell you what they are thinking and feeling when they have a problem? How can the Holy Spirit help you know what to say when someone needs help?

My Radiant Beauty

Worship Me in the beauty of holiness. I created beauty to declare the existence of My holy Being. A magnificent rose, a hauntingly glorious sunset, oceanic splendor—all these things were meant to proclaim My Presence in the world. Most people rush past these proclamations without giving them a second thought. Some people use beauty, especially feminine loveliness, to sell their products.

How precious are My children who are awed by nature's beauty; this opens them up to My holy Presence. Even before you knew Me personally, you responded to My creation with wonder. This is a gift, and it carries responsibility with it. Declare My glorious Being to the world. *The whole earth is full of My radiant beauty—My Glory!*

READ TOGETHER

And they were calling to one another: "Holy, holy, holy is the Lord Almighty; the whole earth is full of his glory."

—Isaiah 6:3

READ MORE: PSALM 29:2 NKJV; 1 SAMUEL 2:2

The Beauty of Creation

The whole of creation declares that I am God. And the beauty of creation declares My Glory.

Open your eyes to the beauty all around you. See the majesty of the mountains, the power of the ocean waves, the details of the tiniest wildflower, the endless colors of the sunset—and know that I am holy God.

So many people rush past these signs of My Presence without even giving them a second thought. Some people just use beauty to sell their products—forgetting all about Me. But I want you to open your eyes to the glory of My creation. Let this awesome beauty draw you into worshiping Me.

Be glad that I am a holy God who created such a beautiful world. And use the glory of My creation to tell others about Me. The whole earth is full of My shining beauty—*My Glory!*

TALK TOGETHER

Take a moment to step outside and look at the world around you—the skies, the trees, the birds. What does God's creation tell you about Him? What does it tell you about His love and care for you?

My Abundant Blessings

THIS IS A TIME OF ABUNDANCE in your life. *Your cup runneth over* with blessings. After plodding uphill for many weeks, you are now traipsing through lush meadows drenched in warm sunshine. I want you to enjoy to the full this time of ease and refreshment. I delight in providing it for you.

Sometimes My children hesitate to receive My good gifts with open hands. Feelings of false guilt creep in, telling them they don't deserve to be so richly blessed. This is nonsense-thinking because no one deserves anything from Me. My kingdom is not about earning and deserving; it's about believing and receiving.

When a child of Mine balks at accepting My gifts, I am deeply grieved. When you receive My abundant blessings with a grateful heart, I rejoice. My pleasure in giving and your pleasure in receiving flow together in joyous harmony.

READ TOGETHER

Thou preparest a table before me in the presence of mine enemies: thou anointest my head with oil; my cup runneth over.

—PSALM 23:5 KJV

READ MORE: JOHN 3:16; LUKE 11:9–10; ROMANS 8:32

You Can't Earn My Blessings

This is a time of plenty in your life. Your cup overflows with blessings. Enjoy this time—it is My gift to you.

Don't feel guilty when everything is going well. Don't turn away from My blessings because you think you don't deserve to be so blessed. That is nonsense. The truth is that no one deserves anything from Me. My kingdom is not about earning blessings. And life with Me is not some sort of game in which you earn points to buy prizes. Good behavior doesn't buy blessings.

Instead of trying to work for My blessings, I want you to receive them thankfully. I give you good gifts because I love to see your joy when you receive them. So open your hands and your heart, and accept My blessings gratefully. This brings Joy to you *and* to Me!

TALK TOGETHER

What are some of your greatest blessings? Are you blessed only when good things are happening? How can you remember to thank God always for the many blessings in your life?

You Are a New Creation

I am the Risen One who shines upon you always. You worship a living Deity, not some idolatrous, man-made image. Your relationship with Me is meant to be vibrant and challenging as I invade more and more areas of your life. Do not fear change, for I am making you a *new creation, with old things passing away and new things continually on the horizon.* When you cling to old ways and sameness, you resist My work within you. I want you to embrace all that I am doing in your life, finding your security in Me alone.

It is easy to make an idol of routine, finding security within the boundaries you build around your life. Although each day contains twenty-four hours, every single one presents a unique set of circumstances. Don't try to force-fit today into yesterday's mold. Instead, ask Me to open your eyes so you can find all I have prepared for you in this precious day of Life.

READ TOGETHER

Therefore, if anyone is in Christ, he is a new creation; the old has gone, the new has come!

—2 Corinthians 5:17

Read More: Matthew 28:5–7

A New You

I came to earth, was crucified, and then rose from the grave so that I could create a *new you*. A "you" who isn't stuck in a boring routine, who doesn't worry what others think, who isn't afraid to try new things.

I want you to have an exciting life, full of adventure and challenge. I have lots of plans for you; I want you to do great things for My kingdom. First, though, you have to give Me control of your old life. Let Me have your old worries, your old struggles, your old temptations and sins. I will throw them all away so that I can work in your life.

Change can be frightening, but trust Me. I have great plans for this day—and every day—of your life.

TALK TOGETHER

How is the "new you" different from the "old you"? Are there old worries, struggles, temptations, or sins that you need to give to Jesus? Ask Jesus to take away these things from your old life and give you a new life in Him.

THE SHIELD OF FAITH

SPENDING TIME alone with Me is essential for your well-being. It is not a luxury or an option; it is a necessity. Therefore, do not feel guilty about taking time to be with Me. Remember that Satan is *the accuser of believers*. He delights in heaping guilt feelings upon you, especially when you are enjoying My Presence. When you feel Satan's arrows of accusation, you are probably on the right track. Use your *shield of faith* to protect yourself from him. Talk with Me about what you are experiencing, and ask Me to show you the way forward. *Resist the devil, and he will flee from you. Come near to Me, and I will come near to you.*

READ TOGETHER

In addition to all this, take up the shield of faith, with which you can extinguish all the flaming arrows of the evil one.

—EPHESIANS 6:16

READ MORE: REVELATION 12:10; JAMES 4:7–8

Take Up Your Shield

There is a battle going on every day—a battle for your mind. And Satan has an unlimited supply of arrows. His arrows are the lies that he whispers to you, trying to weaken your faith. His arrows say, "No one loves you," "Even Jesus wouldn't forgive that," "There's no hope for you," "You are so worthless" . . . lie after lie after lie.

Protect yourself with your shield of faith. When you feel the sting of one of Satan's lies, come to Me and hear My truth. The truth is, I love you so much that I died for you. There is nothing you can do that I won't forgive. In Me, there is always hope. And you are My own special creation, always precious to Me.

Take up your shield of faith. Stand up to the devil, and he will run away from you. Come close to Me, and I will come close to you.

TALK TOGETHER

What lies does the devil try to get you to believe? What does God's Word say about those lies? How does the shield of faith protect you from the evil one's lies?

SEEK TO PLEASE ME

SEEK TO PLEASE ME above all else. Let that goal be your focal point as you go through this day. Such a mind-set will protect you from scattering your energy to the winds. The free will I bestowed on you comes with awesome responsibility. Each day presents you with choice after choice. Many of these decisions you ignore and thus make by default. Without a focal point to guide you, you can easily lose your way. That's why it is so important to stay in communication with Me, living in thankful awareness of My Presence.

You inhabit a fallen, disjointed world, where things are constantly unraveling around the edges. Only a vibrant relationship with Me can keep you from coming unraveled too.

READ TOGETHER

Whatever you do, work at it with all your heart, as working for the Lord, not for men, since you know that you will receive an inheritance from the Lord as a reward. It is the Lord Christ you are serving.
—COLOSSIANS 3:23–24

READ MORE: MATTHEW 6:33; JOHN 8:29

Working for Me

Every day you are faced with choice after choice. When you're trying to make decisions, you need a good goal to guide you. So seek to please Me in all your choices—in all that you do.

You know that in order to please Me you need to spend time with Me. Worship, prayer, praise, and Bible study—these are things that make Me smile.

But pleasing Me isn't just about the things you do with Me. It's also about the things you do for Me. From the big things like helping the sick, giving to the poor, and being a friend to the friendless, to the everyday things like emptying the dishwasher for your mom, taking out the trash for your dad, and being respectful—do everything for Me. It may seem like you are working for others, but you are really working for Me. So do the best you can, knowing I'll be with you in all of it.

TALK TOGETHER

How is working for the Lord different from working for people? If you make pleasing Jesus your goal, what does that change in your life?

Sit and Spend Time with Me

Relax in My healing Presence. As you spend time with Me, your thoughts tend to jump ahead to today's plans and problems. Bring your mind back to Me for refreshment and renewal. Let the Light of My Presence soak into you as you focus your thoughts on Me. Thus I equip you to face whatever the day brings. This sacrifice of time pleases Me and strengthens you. Do not skimp on our time together. Resist the clamor of tasks waiting to be done. *You have chosen what is better, and it will not be taken away from you.*

READ TOGETHER

She had a sister called Mary, who sat at the Lord's feet listening to what he said. But Martha was distracted by all the preparations that had to be made. She came to him and asked, "Lord, don't you care that my sister has left me to do the work by myself? Tell her to help me!" "Martha, Martha," the Lord answered, "you are worried and upset about many things, but only one thing is needed. Mary has chosen what is better, and it will not be taken away from her."

—Luke 10:39–42

Read More: Psalm 89:15; Psalm 105:4

Choose Me

You are so very busy. But I want you to stop for a minute. Put down the game, hang up the phone, turn off the computer. Spend some time with Me.

Even now your thoughts are racing ahead to today's plans and problems. But put those thoughts and worries aside. Just think about Me and how much I love you. I know exactly what is going to happen in your life today. Don't worry. I will give you everything you need to face your day.

Please don't skimp on our time together. The computer and the telephone and the homework will still be there when our time is through. Choose Me first—and the blessings I give you will not be taken away.

TALK TOGETHER

Why is time with Jesus so important? Can you tell a difference on days when you spend time with Jesus and on days when you don't remember to spend time with Jesus? What will you do to make sure your day includes time for Him?

Waiting in God's Presence

I am working on your behalf. Bring Me all your concerns, including your dreams. Talk with Me about everything, letting the Light of My Presence shine on your hopes and plans. Spend time allowing My Light to infuse your dreams with life, gradually transforming them into reality. This is a very practical way of collaborating with Me. I, the Creator of the universe, have deigned to cocreate with you. Do not try to hurry this process. If you want to work with Me, you have to accept My time frame. Hurry is not in My nature. Abraham and Sarah had to wait many years for the fulfillment of My promise, a son. How their long wait intensified their enjoyment of this child! *Faith is the assurance of things hoped for, perceiving as real fact what is not revealed to the senses.*

READ TOGETHER

Now faith is the assurance (the confirmation, the title deed) of the things [we] hope for, being the proof of things [we] do not see and the conviction of their reality [faith perceiving as real fact what is not revealed to the senses].

—Hebrews 11:1 AMP

Read More: Psalm 36:9; Genesis 21:1–7

Faith Is Knowing

Every moment of every day, I am working for your good. So bring Me all your worries and fear. Talk with Me about everything. Let the Light of My Presence chase your shadows away.

Bring Me your hopes and dreams too. Let's work on them together, changing them little by little from wishes to reality.

All this takes time. Don't try to take shortcuts or rush the process. When you work with Me, you must learn to accept My timing. Remember how long Abraham and Sarah waited for a son? But when Isaac finally came, their joy was even greater because of their long wait.

Faith is *knowing* I will keep My promises—believing that things you are hoping for are as real as things you can already see.

TALK TOGETHER

Does knowing that God's timing is perfect make it easier for you to trust His timing? What if His timing is different from your own? Why should you trust God's timing—*especially* when it's different from your own?

THE POWER OF WORDS

WATCH YOUR WORDS DILIGENTLY. Words have such great power to bless or to wound. When you speak carelessly or negatively, you damage others as well as yourself. This ability to verbalize is an awesome privilege, granted only to those I created in My image. You need help in wielding this mighty power responsibly.

Though the world applauds quick-witted retorts, My instructions about communication are quite different: *Be quick to listen, slow to speak, and slow to become angry.* Ask My Spirit to help you whenever you speak. I have trained you to pray—"Help me, Holy Spirit"—before answering the phone, and you have seen the benefits of this discipline. Simply apply the same discipline to communicating with people around you. If they are silent, pray before speaking to them. If they are talking, pray before responding. These are split-second prayers, but they put you in touch with My Presence. In this way, your speaking comes under the control of My Spirit. As positive speech patterns replace your negative ones, the increase in your Joy will amaze you.

READ TOGETHER

Do not let any unwholesome talk come out of your mouths, but only what is helpful for building others up according to their needs, that it may benefit those who listen.

—EPHESIANS 4:29

READ MORE: PROVERBS 12:18; JAMES 1:19

Sticks and Stones

The saying, "Sticks and stones may break my bones, but words will never hurt me," just simply isn't true. Words can cut deeper than any knife. And the wounds they leave behind may never heal.

The world praises people who say "clever" things—even if they embarrass and hurt others. But that is *not* the kind of person I want you to be. Your words are powerful tools. I want you to use them to build up those around you, not tear them down.

I know you get angry and frustrated at times, but don't say the first thing that pops into your mind. Pray first! Before you pick up the phone, pray. Before you answer someone else's angry words, pray. Before you say *anything*, pray! A simple, split-second prayer—"Help me, Jesus"—is all it takes to put your words under My control.

TALK TOGETHER

Have words ever hurt you? Think of a time when your words hurt someone—when you said something you wish you had not. What could you have said instead?

Discern My Voice

I LOVE YOU FOR WHO YOU ARE, not for what you do. Many voices vie for control of your mind, especially when you sit in silence. You must learn to discern what is My voice and what is not. Ask My Spirit to give you this discernment. Many of My children run around in circles, trying to obey the various voices directing their lives. This results in fragmented, frustrating patterns of living. Do not fall into this trap. Walk closely with Me each moment, listening for My directives and enjoying My Companionship. Refuse to let other voices tie you up in knots. *My sheep know My voice and follow Me wherever I lead.*

READ TOGETHER

"When he has brought out all his own, he goes on ahead of them, and his sheep follow him because they know his voice."

—JOHN 10:4

READ MORE: EPHESIANS 4:1–6

Listen for My Voice

There are lots of voices out there trying to get your attention. Friends, television—and yes, even the devil. They all try to tell you what is important and how you should act. And often, they all say something different. If you listen to all those voices, you will end up running in circles and getting nowhere—like a puppy chasing its tail!

Learn to listen for *My* voice. Learn to tell My voice apart from all the others. How is that possible? *Pray.* Ask My Spirit to help you hear My voice above all the others. Listen closely to what I have to say, and then follow Me wherever I lead.

TALK TOGETHER

What does a shepherd do for his sheep? If we are like sheep, who is our Good Shepherd? How can we let the Good Shepherd guide us? How do we know how to follow Jesus?

The Mind Controlled by the Spirit

Let Me control your mind. The mind is the most restless, unruly part of mankind. Long after you have learned the discipline of holding your tongue, your thoughts defy your will and set themselves up against Me. Man is the pinnacle of My creation, and the human mind is wondrously complex. I risked all by granting you freedom to think for yourself. This is godlike privilege, forever setting you apart from animals and robots. *I made you in My image*, precariously close to deity.

Though My blood has fully redeemed you, your mind is the last bastion of rebellion. Open yourself to My radiant Presence, letting My Light permeate your thinking. *When My Spirit is controlling your mind, you are filled with Life and Peace.*

READ TOGETHER

Then God said, "Let us make man in our image, in our likeness, and let them rule over the fish of the sea and the birds of the air, over the livestock, over all the earth, and over all the creatures that move along the ground." So God created man in his own image, in the image of God he created him; male and female he created them.

—Genesis 1:26–27

Read More: Psalm 8:5 nkjv; Romans 8:6

Your Amazing Mind

I created you in My own image. You are the best of My creation. I gave you a mind that is capable of amazing, creative thoughts. And I risked everything by giving you the freedom to think for yourself. Your wonderful human mind makes you totally different from animals and robots.

I could have created you so that you *had* to always love Me and seek Me. But I wanted you to use your mind to *choose* loving and seeking Me.

Your mind is amazing. It can imagine, it can dream, and it can also rebel. Bring your mind and thoughts to Me. Let Me take away the anger, the doubts, the rebellion—and give you Love, Faith, and Peace.

TALK TOGETHER

God created your mind, and then He allowed you to think for yourself. How is your mind a wonderful gift? Why do you think God allows you to *choose* to love Him—instead of making you love Him?

ENJOY MY PRESENCE

I AM THE FIRM FOUNDATION on which you can dance and sing and celebrate My Presence. This is My high and holy calling for you; receive it as a precious gift. *Glorifying and enjoying Me* is a higher priority than maintaining a tidy, structured life. Give up your striving to keep everything under control—an impossible task and a waste of precious energy.

My guidance for each of My children is unique. That's why listening to Me is so vital for your well-being. Let me prepare you for the day that awaits you and point you in the right direction. I am with you continually, so don't be intimidated by fear. Though it stalks you, it cannot harm you, as long as you cling to My hand. Keep your eyes on Me, enjoying Peace in My Presence.

READ TOGETHER

But let all who take refuge in you be glad; let them ever sing for joy. Spread your protection over them, that those who love your name may rejoice in you.

—PSALM 5:11

READ MORE: EPHESIANS 3:20–21;
JUDE VV. 24–25; JOSHUA 1:5

Shout for Joy!

Sing! Dance! Shout for joy because I am your God! There is no greater reason to celebrate.

Sing of My Love and forgiveness wherever you go. Dance and shout for joy because you serve a God who loves and treasures you.

Live your life in praise to Me. Let the words you speak and the things you do bring Me Glory. I am with you always, so don't let fear silence your praise. Keep your eyes on Me, and I will keep you going in the right direction. So sing, dance, and shout for joy!

TALK TOGETHER

I am your God! There is no greater reason to celebrate! Explain how this is true. How can you celebrate God in your life?

GOD WITH YOU

I AM *GOD WITH YOU,* for all time and throughout eternity. Don't let the familiarity of that concept numb its impact on your consciousness. My perpetual Presence with you can be a continual source of Joy, springing up and flowing out in streams of abundant Life. Let your mind reverberate with meanings of My Names: Jesus, *the Lord saves*; and Immanuel, *God with us.* Strive to remain conscious of My Presence even in your busiest moments. Talk with Me about whatever delights you, whatever upsets you, whatever is on your mind. These tiny steps of daily discipline, taken one after the other, will keep you close to Me on the path of Life.

READ TOGETHER

"She will give birth to a son, and you are to give him the name Jesus, because he will save his people from their sins. . . . The virgin will be with child and will give birth to a son, and they will call him Immanuel"—which means, "God with us."

—MATTHEW 1:21, 23

READ MORE: JOHN 10:10 NKJV; ACTS 2:28

Who I Am

I am God with you. You hear about this so often in church. But don't ever let it become ordinary. Don't ever stop living in awe of Me.

Stop and think for a moment about who I am. My Name is Jesus. It means "the Lord saves." I save you. I save you from the troubles and despair of this world. And I save you from your sins for all eternity.

I am also Immanuel, which means "God with us." *God with you.* I am always with you, and I'm always waiting to hear from you. Tell me about whatever makes you happy, whatever upsets you, whatever is on your mind.

Don't ever get so used to Me that you forget the wonder of who I am or the Joy of knowing Me—the God and Creator of all the universe.

TALK TOGETHER

Jesus means "the Lord saves," and Immanuel means "God with us." What do these names tell you about your God and what He wants to do for you? Why is that important?

Don't Try to Fix Everything

Problems are part of life. They are inescapable, woven into the very fabric of this fallen world. You tend to go into problem-solving mode all too readily, acting as if you have the capacity to fix everything. This is a habitual response, so automatic that it bypasses your conscious thinking. Not only does this habit frustrate you, it also distances you from Me.

Do not let fixing things be your top priority. You are ever so limited in your capacity to correct all that is wrong in the world around you. Don't weigh yourself down with responsibilities that are not your own. Instead, make your relationship with Me your primary concern. Talk with Me about whatever is on your mind, seeking My perspective on the situation. Rather than trying to fix everything that comes to your attention, ask Me to show you what is truly important. Remember that you are *en route* to heaven, and let your problems fade in the Light of eternity.

READ TOGETHER

But our citizenship is in heaven. And we eagerly await a Savior from there, the Lord Jesus Christ, who, by the power that enables him to bring everything under his control, will transform our lowly bodies so that they will be like his glorious body.

—Philippians 3:20–21

Read More: Psalm 32:8; Luke 10:41–42

Heavenly Light

There are a lot of things in this world that need fixing. There are a lot of things in *your* world that need fixing: broken promises, broken relationships, and much more. But you don't have to be the fix-it person. In fact, you *can't* be. You're only human.

Still, that doesn't stop you from trying. When you see something wrong, you tend to jump right into problem solving. But that is not your main responsibility in life. Your main responsibility is your relationship with Me. If a problem enters your day, talk with Me about it. Ask for My thoughts on it. Rather than just jumping in and trying to fix everything, ask Me to show you what is truly important.

Remember, this world is only temporary, and you are just passing through it. Your true home is in heaven—and even your biggest problems fade in the heavenly Light of eternity.

TALK TOGETHER

Problems can make this world seem dark. But even the darkest problems fade when the Light of Heaven shines on them. Why is that? Have you seen this happen in your own life? Will you have problems in heaven?

WHISPER MY NAME

WHENEVER YOU FEEL DISTANT from Me, whisper My Name in loving trust. This simple prayer can restore your awareness of My Presence.

My Name is constantly abused in the world, where people use it as a curse word. This verbal assault reaches all the way to heaven; every word is heard and recorded. When you trustingly whisper My Name, My aching ears are soothed. The grating rancor of the world's blasphemies cannot compete with a trusting child's utterance: "Jesus." The power of My Name to bless both you and Me is beyond your understanding.

READ TOGETHER

Salvation is found in no one else, for there is no other name under heaven given to men by which we must be saved.

—ACTS 4:12

READ MORE: PROVERBS 18:10; JOHN 16:24

My Name

My Name is constantly abused in this world. Some people use it carelessly, without even realizing they are talking about the Lord of lords. Other people use it as a curse word, which is an attack on who I am. Every time My Name is used, it is recorded in heaven.

So when you say My Name in prayer, when you call out My Name in praise, and when you whisper My Name in trust, My aching heart is soothed. All the curses of the world are drowned out by your loving whisper: "Jesus." When you speak My Name in these ways, both you *and* I are blessed.

TALK TOGETHER

Jesus hears you every time you say His name. Do these words make you feel uncomfortable or happy about how you use Jesus' name? Why is His the most important name? How can you show honor and love for Jesus' name?

GREEN PASTURES

COME TO ME with all your weaknesses: physical, emotional, and spiritual. Rest in the comfort of My Presence, remembering that *nothing is impossible with Me.*

Pry your mind away from your problems so you can focus your attention on Me. Recall that I am *able to do immeasurably more than all you ask or imagine.* Instead of trying to direct Me to do this and that, seek to attune yourself to what I am *already* doing.

When anxiety attempts to wedge its way into your thoughts, remind yourself that *I am your Shepherd.* The bottom line is that I am taking care of you; therefore, you needn't be afraid of anything. Rather than trying to maintain control over your life, abandon yourself to My will. Though this may feel frightening—even dangerous—the safest place to be is in My will.

READ TOGETHER

The LORD is my shepherd, I shall not be in want. He makes me lie down in green pastures, he leads me beside quiet waters, he restores my soul. He guides me in paths of righteousness for his name's sake. Even though I walk through the valley of the shadow of death, I will fear no evil, for you are with me; your rod and your staff, they comfort me.

—PSALM 23:1–4

READ MORE: LUKE 1:37; EPHESIANS 3:20–21

I Am Your Shepherd

A shepherd cares for his sheep. When they are hungry, he leads them to food. When they are thirsty, he finds water. When they are hurt, he takes care of them. When wild animals attack, he protects them. When they are surrounded by the darkness of the night, he comforts them.

I am your Shepherd, and you are My most precious sheep. I am taking care of you, so you don't have to be afraid of anything—ever. Your job is to follow Me. A sheep does not lead the shepherd, so you need to give Me control of your life. Though this may feel scary at times—even dangerous—the safest place to be is right next to Me.

TALK TOGETHER

Read Psalm 23. How does a shepherd keep his sheep safe? How is the Lord your Shepherd? How is being right next to Jesus the safest place to be?

Your Friend and Lord

I AM WITH YOU and all around you, encircling you in golden rays of Light. I always behold you Face to face. Not one of your thoughts escapes My notice. Because I am infinite, I am able to love you as if you and I were the only ones in the universe.

Walk with Me in intimate Love-steps, but do not lose sight of My Majesty. I desire to be your closest Friend, yet I am also your sovereign Lord. I created your brain with capacity to know Me as Friend and Lord simultaneously. The human mind is the pinnacle of My creation, but so few use it for its primary purpose—knowing Me. I communicate continually through My Spirit, My Word, and My creation. Only humans are capable of receiving Me and responding to My Presence. You are indeed *fearfully and wonderfully made*!

READ TOGETHER

I praise you because I am fearfully and wonderfully made; your works are wonderful, I know that full well.

—PSALM 139:14

READ MORE: PSALM 34:4–6; 2 PETER 1:16–17; JOHN 17:3

My Definition of Wonderful

I created *you*, not just humans in general. Every detail, every feature of yours, was lovingly and carefully formed by Me. *And you are wonderful!*

This world will tell you that you need to look a certain way, talk a certain way, and live a certain way in order to be wonderful. Just look at any magazine, and you will see the world's definition of wonderful—thanks to digital photography and a few tweaks here and there on the computer. But remember that this world is ruled by the father of lies. And one of his biggest whoppers is that only certain people are truly special.

All My children are wonderful—each in his or her own unique way. Just look in the mirror, and you will see *My* definition of wonderful.

TALK TOGETHER

You are made in "an amazing and wonderful way" by an amazing and wonderful God. Think of three things about how God made you that are awesome. How can you use your mind, your body, and your talents to show others how amazing and wonderful God is?

Begin Each Day with Me

Seek My Face at the beginning of your day. This practice enables you to "put Me on" and "wear Me" throughout the day. Most people put on clothes soon after arising from bed. Similarly, the sooner you "put Me on" by communicating with Me, the better prepared you are for whatever comes your way.

To "wear Me" is essentially to have My mind: to think My thoughts. Ask the Holy Spirit to control your thinking; be transformed by this renewal within you. Thus you are well-equipped to face whatever people and situations I bring your way. Clothing your mind in Me is your best preparation for each day. This discipline brings Joy and Peace to you and those around you.

READ TOGETHER

Rather, clothe yourselves with the Lord Jesus Christ, and do not think about how to gratify the desires of the sinful nature.

—Romans 13:14

Read More: Psalm 27:8 nkjv;
1 Corinthians 2:16; Colossians 3:12

Put Me On

Every morning you put on the clothes you need for that day. A jacket for cooler days. Boots for rain. Sweats for exercising. Putting on the right clothes prepares you for your day.

Clothes take care of the outside, but what about the inside? I have a suggestion: Put *Me* on. Wear *Me*. This will prepare you for your day.

How? "Put Me on" by talking to Me first thing in the morning. And then "wear Me" throughout the day by keeping Me in your thoughts. Keep checking in, because things change. Just as a change in the weather might call for a change in clothes, a change in your world might call for a change from Me. Maybe this morning you needed encouragement, but now a little forgiveness is what you need.

So clothe yourself with Me—it's the best way to start your day.

TALK TOGETHER

Think about what clothes do for you—they protect you, they keep you comfortable, and they can even help you do the things you need to do (like a spacesuit or a diving suit). How does "wearing" Jesus provide for you, protect you, and help you do what you need to do?

Unhurried

I am preparing you for what is on the road ahead, just around the bend. Take time to be still in My Presence so that I can strengthen you. The busier you become, the more you need this time apart with Me. So many people think that time spent with Me is a luxury they cannot afford. As a result, they live and work in their own strength—until that becomes depleted. Then they either cry out to Me for help or turn away in bitterness.

How much better it is to walk close to Me, depending on My strength and trusting Me in every situation. If you live in this way, you will *do* less but *accomplish* far more. Your unhurried pace of living will stand out in this rush-crazed age. Some people may deem you lazy, but many more will be blessed by your peacefulness. Walk in the Light with Me, and you will reflect Me to the watching world.

READ TOGETHER

Since ancient times no one has heard, no ear has perceived, no eye has seen any God besides you, who acts on behalf of those who wait for him.

—Isaiah 64:4

READ More: John 15:5; Psalm 36:9

While You Wait

Busy. Busy. Busy. Many of My children are so very busy, they think they just don't have time to spend with Me. So they live and work in their own strength. And when that runs out, they either cry out to Me for help or turn away angrily.

But it's so much better to live close to Me all along—depending on My Strength and trusting Me for help. If you live this way, you will *do* less but actually get more of the important things done.

When you take time for Me, your unhurried way of living will stand out in this rush, rush world. Some people may think you are lazy, but many more will be blessed by your peacefulness.

So make time to wait with Me, and I will *work for you* while you wait.

TALK TOGETHER

It doesn't seem logical, but you will actually get more of the important things done when you slow down and spend time with Jesus. How is this true? Create a plan to spend more time with Jesus, and then encourage one another to carry out your plans. How will your life look different if you slow down your activities and spend time with Jesus?

A Thankful Heart

Come to Me with a thankful heart so that you can enjoy My Presence. This is the day that I have made. I want you to rejoice *today*, refusing to worry about tomorrow. Search for all that I have prepared for you, anticipating abundant blessings and accepting difficulties as they come. I can weave miracles into the most mundane day if you keep your focus on Me.

Come to Me with all your needs, knowing that *My glorious riches* are a more-than-adequate supply. Stay in continual communication with Me so that you can live above your circumstances even while you are in the midst of them. *Present your requests to Me with thanksgiving, and My Peace, which surpasses all comprehension, will guard your heart and mind.*

READ TOGETHER

Be anxious for nothing, but in everything by prayer and supplication with thanksgiving let your requests be made known to God. And the peace of God, which surpasses all comprehension, will guard your hearts and your minds in Christ Jesus.

—Philippians 4:6–7 NASB

Read More: Psalm 118:24; Philippians 4:19

No More Boring Days

Come to Me with a thankful heart. I have made this day for you so that you can enjoy My Presence in it. Don't worry about tomorrow. Rejoice in today. Look for the many blessings and miracles that I have put into this day. If you look for My Presence in your life, you will find it.

Come to Me with all your needs, big and small, knowing that I will take care of you. When you are not worried about what is happening in your life, then you are free to truly live. I want to give you that freedom. Turn your heart over to Me and I will fill it with peace and joy. And there will be no more boring days!

TALK TOGETHER

Which days are a gift from the Lord? How does having a thankful heart help you better enjoy that gift? Which of your worries should you tell Jesus about?

A Love Song for You

Listen to the love song that I am continually singing to you. *I take great delight in you. I rejoice over you with singing.* The voices of the world are a cacophony of chaos, pulling you this way and that. Don't listen to those voices; challenge them with My Word. Learn to take minibreaks from the world, finding a place to be still in My Presence and listen to My voice.

There is immense hidden treasure to be found through listening to Me. Though I pour out blessings upon you always, some of My richest blessings have to be actively sought. I love to reveal Myself to you, and your seeking heart opens you up to receive more of My disclosure. *Ask and it will be given to you; seek and you will find; knock and the door will be opened to you.*

READ TOGETHER

"The Lord your God is with you, he is mighty to save. He will take great delight in you, he will quiet you with his love, he will rejoice over you with singing."

—Zephaniah 3:17

Read More: Matthew 17:5; Matthew 7:7

Hear My Song

Do you hear that? I am singing you a song. It is a love song. You give Me so much joy that I just have to sing!

You won't hear My song like you would a song on the radio. But listen with your heart, and you'll hear Me. I know there is noise all around you. Voices pulling you this way and that way. Don't listen to them! Take a break from all the noise. Find a quiet place to be still in My Presence and listen to My voice.

That beautiful bird's song? It's saying I love you. That whisper of wind through the trees? It's singing My Joy that you are with Me. Even the patter of the rain says you delight Me. Listen to My song—it's like no other music you'll ever hear.

TALK TOGETHER

Do you remember when you were little and someone sang over you at bedtime? Did you know that God sings over you? Read Zephaniah 3:17. What do you think God is singing over you?

Lean on Me

GROW STRONG IN YOUR WEAKNESS. Some of My children I've gifted with abundant strength and stamina. Others, like you, have received the humble gift of frailty. Your fragility is not a punishment, nor does it indicate lack of faith. On the contrary, weak ones like you must live by faith, depending on Me to get you through the day. I am developing your ability to trust Me, to *lean on Me rather than on your understanding*. Your natural preference is to plan out your day, knowing what will happen when. My preference is for you to depend on Me continually, trusting Me to guide you and strengthen you as needed. This is how you grow strong in your weakness.

READ TOGETHER

Do you not know? Have you not heard? The LORD is the everlasting God, the Creator of the ends of the earth. He will not grow tired or weary, and his understanding no one can fathom. He gives strength to the weary and increases the power of the weak. Even youths grow tired and weary, and young men stumble and fall; but those who hope in the LORD will renew their strength. They will soar on wings like eagles; they will run and not grow weary, they will walk and not be faint.

—ISAIAH 40:28–31

READ MORE: JAMES 4:13–15; PROVERBS 3:5 AMP

Have You Heard?

Have you heard? I use your weaknesses to make you stronger.

That sounds backward, doesn't it? The world says that the strong are those who don't have any weaknesses; the strong are the people who do it all on their own, who rely on their own strength and smarts. But I tell you that there will come a time when those people will run out of strength and their own wisdom will fail them.

My Way is different. I use your unexpected problems to urge you to seek My guidance. Your weaknesses are not punishment. Rather, struggles are a gift that helps you learn to depend on Me. I want you to trust Me and lean on Me—rather than on your own understanding.

When you lean on Me, you are truly strong. Because My Strength never runs out, and My wisdom never fails.

TALK TOGETHER

Do you ever get tired? Do you know anyone who is stronger than you? Of course you do! God. How can your strong God take care of you?

Everyday Blessings

WHEN I GIVE YOU no special guidance, stay where you are. Concentrate on doing your everyday tasks in awareness of My Presence with you. The Joy of My Presence will shine on you as you do everything for Me. Thus you invite Me into every aspect of your life. Through collaborating with Me in all things, you allow My Life to merge with yours. This is the secret of not only joyful living but of victorious living. I designed you to depend on Me moment by moment, recognizing that *apart from Me you can do nothing.*

Be thankful for quiet days, when nothing special seems to be happening. Instead of being bored by the lack of action, use times of routine to seek My Face. Although this is an invisible transaction, it speaks volumes in spiritual realms. Moreover, you are richly blessed when you walk trustingly with Me through the routines of your day.

READ TOGETHER

"I am the vine; you are the branches. If a man remains in me and I in him, he will bear much fruit; apart from me you can do nothing."
—JOHN 15:5

READ MORE: COLOSSIANS 3:23; PSALM 105:4

Ordinary Days

Some of your days are full of action, adventure, and challenge. Other days are . . . well, ordinary. But don't let yourself be bored. Choose to be thankful for quiet days, and then use them to spend extra time with Me.

Invite Me into your everyday tasks. Do everything as if you were doing it for Me . . . yes, even making the bed, finishing up your homework, and all the other ordinary stuff of life. And through it all, enjoy simply being in My company.

When you go through the activities of your day side-by-side with Me, My Life becomes woven together with yours. This means you and I are so closely connected that My own Life flows into you—and through you into the world around you. And that is the real secret of having a joy-filled life—even on ordinary days.

TALK TOGETHER

Can you think of one really happy day? Do you know you can have joy every day? Who do you invite to be with you every day? That's right, Jesus!

Cease Striving

Relax in My healing, holy Presence. *Be still* while I transform your heart and mind. *Let go* of cares and worries so that you can receive My Peace. *Cease striving, and know that I am God.*

Do not be like Pharisees who multiplied regulations, creating their own form of "godliness." They got so wrapped up in their own rules that they lost sight of Me. Even today, man-made rules about how to live the Christian life enslave many people. Their focus is on their performance, rather than on Me.

It is through knowing Me intimately that you become like Me. This requires spending time alone with Me. *Let go, relax, be still, and know that I am God.*

READ TOGETHER

Dear friends, now we are children of God, and what we will be has not yet been made known. But we know that when he appears, we shall be like him, for we shall see him as he is.

—1 John 3:2

Read More: Psalm 46:10 nasb; Matthew 23:13

You Are My Child

I am God, and you are My child. And like so many parents on earth, I want you to grow up to be like Me. To become more like Me, you need to spend time with Me. Relax in My Presence, while I work in your heart and mind. Let go of cares and worries so that you can receive My Peace. *Be still, and know that I am God.*

Don't worry about what others think. Don't worry about what's "cool" or "in." And don't be like the Pharisees in the Bible. They got so wrapped up in their own rules that they lost sight of Me.

Keep your eyes on Me, and remember how much I love you. This helps you love Me and also love others with *My* Love.

TALK TOGETHER

Who is in your family? Do your parents want you to grow up and be like your best friend? Like your brother or sister? Like the dog? No! They want you to grow up to be more like Jesus. How can you do that?

Setbacks or Opportunities?

Every time something thwarts your plans or desires, use that as a reminder to communicate with Me. This practice has several benefits. The first is obvious: Talking with Me blesses you and strengthens our relationship. Another benefit is that disappointments, instead of dragging you down, are transformed into opportunities for good. This transformation removes the sting from difficult circumstances, making it possible to be joyful in the midst of adversity.

Begin by practicing this discipline in all the little disappointments of daily life. It is often these minor setbacks that draw you away from My Presence. When you reframe *setbacks* as *opportunities*, you find that you gain much more than you have lost. It is only after much training that you can accept major losses in this positive way. But it is possible to attain the perspective of the apostle Paul, who wrote: *Compared to the surpassing greatness of knowing Christ Jesus, I consider everything I once treasured to be as insignificant as rubbish.*

READ TOGETHER

But whatever was to my profit I now consider loss for the sake of Christ. What is more, I consider everything a loss compared to the surpassing greatness of knowing Christ Jesus my Lord, for whose sake I have lost all things. I consider them rubbish, that I may gain Christ.

—Philippians 3:7–8

Read More: Proverbs 19:21; Colossians 4:2

Count It as Garbage

When your plans are messed up, talk to Me about it. Talking with Me blesses you and strengthens our friendship. Also, I take the sting out of your disappointment by making something good come of it. So you can be joyful, even when things are going wrong. But it takes practice.

Start by bringing Me small things—the bad grade, the rained-out game. Even small disappointments can focus your thoughts on yourself instead of Me. But when you talk with Me, you see that the things you've lost are nothing compared to the wonders of knowing Me.

You'll need a lot of practice before you can trust Me with big disappointments. But if you keep at it, someday even the greatest things of this world will seem like garbage compared to the Joy of knowing Me—your Savior, Lord, and Friend.

TALK TOGETHER

Were you ever disappointed because someone didn't share with you? Were you ever disappointed that you didn't win a game? How can you have joy even when you face a disappointment?

STOP COMPARING YOURSELF

STOP JUDGING AND EVALUATING YOURSELF, for this is not your role. Above all, stop comparing yourself with other people. This produces feelings of pride or inferiority, sometimes a mixture of both. I lead each of My children along a path that is uniquely tailor-made for him or her. Comparing is not only wrong; it is also meaningless.

Don't look for affirmation in the wrong places: your own evaluations or those of other people. The only source of real affirmation is My unconditional Love. Many believers perceive Me as an unpleasable Judge, angrily searching out their faults and failures. Nothing could be farther from the truth! I died for your sins so that I might *clothe you in My garments of salvation*. This is how I see you: *radiant in My robe of righteousness*. When I discipline you, it is never in anger or disgust; it is to prepare you for face-to-Face fellowship with Me throughout all eternity. Immerse yourself in My loving Presence. Be receptive to My affirmation, which flows continually from the throne of grace.

READ TOGETHER

I will rejoice greatly in the LORD, my soul will exult in my God; for He has clothed me with garments of salvation, He has wrapped me with a robe of righteousness, as a bridegroom decks himself with a garland, and as a bride adorns herself with her jewels.

—ISAIAH 61:10 NASB

READ MORE: LUKE 6:37; PROVERBS 3:11–12

A Jewel in My Crown

Stop comparing yourself to other people. When you compare yourself to others, you end up either feeling that you're better than they are, or feeling bad about yourself. Neither of those things is what I want for you.

I created each of My children with unique talents. And I have given each of you your own road to follow. So it is useless to compare yourself to someone else—that person has a completely different path to follow.

When you want to feel good about yourself, remember how much I love you. Remember that I made you just the way I want you to be. And remember that I died so you could have My salvation. You are a jewel in My crown.

TALK TOGETHER

Do you ever compare yourself to others? How do you end up feeling? How does it feel to know that God created you to be *you* and that He has a unique plan for your life?

ALL I HAVE FOR YOU

DRAW NEAR TO ME with a thankful heart, aware that your cup is overflowing with blessings. Gratitude enables you to perceive Me more clearly and to rejoice in our Love-relationship. *Nothing can separate you from My loving Presence!* That is the basis of your security. Whenever you start to feel anxious, remind yourself that your security rests in Me alone, and I am totally trustworthy.

You will never be in control of your life circumstances, but you can relax and trust in My control. Instead of striving for a predictable, safe lifestyle, seek to know Me in greater depth and breadth. I long to make your life a glorious adventure, but you must stop clinging to old ways. I am always doing something new within My beloved ones. Be on the lookout for all that I have prepared for you.

READ TOGETHER

"See, I am doing a new thing! Now it springs up; do you not perceive it? I am making a way in the desert and streams in the wasteland."
—ISAIAH 43:19

READ MORE: ROMANS 8:38–39; PSALM 56:3–4

Jump In with Both Feet

You will never be in complete control of your life. It just isn't possible. You want to feel completely safe and secure. But even if you plan out every detail, the world will mess up your plans.

So just stop trying to be in control. Stop trying to make your life completely safe and predictable—*and boring*! Instead, grab My hand and jump in with both feet. I am the One who loves you completely and wants only the very best for you. I want your life to be an amazing adventure—filled with new things. But first you have to let go of old ways of doing things. Then, grab hold of My hand, and look for all the exciting *new* things I've prepared for you!

TALK TOGETHER

Are you ready to go on an adventure with Jesus? Do you know His great adventure for you is to follow Him wherever He leads? Is there anything you need to let go of in order to grab Jesus' hand and go on your great lifelong adventure?

I Understand You

NEVER TAKE FOR GRANTED My intimate nearness. Marvel at the wonder of My continual Presence with you. Even the most ardent human lover cannot be with you always. Nor can another person know the intimacies of your heart, mind, and spirit. *I know everything about you—even the number of hairs on your head.* You don't need to work at revealing yourself to Me.

Many people spend a lifetime or a small fortune searching for someone who understands them. Yet I am freely available to all who call upon My Name, who open their hearts to receive Me as Savior. This simple act of faith is the beginning of a lifelong love story. I, the Lover of your soul, understand you perfectly and love you eternally.

READ TOGETHER

"Indeed, the very hairs of your head are all numbered. Don't be afraid; you are worth more than many sparrows."

—LUKE 12:7

READ MORE: PSALM 145:18 NKJV; JOHN 1:12; ROMANS 10:13

Every Hair on Your Head

Don't ever forget that I know you better than you know yourself—and far better than anyone else knows you. Your parents, your best friend, your brother or sister cannot be with you at all times. But I am. And at every moment I know your every thought, every feeling, every hope and dream. I know every detail about you—right down to how many hairs you have on your head.

Not only do I know you, but I also understand you. I know all the whys and hows that you can't even put into words. I understand what is inside your heart.

Many people spend their whole lives searching for someone who can truly understand them. But all you have to do is call on My Name—opening your heart to Me. This simple act of faith is all it takes. I understand you perfectly, and I love you forever.

TALK TOGETHER

Jesus knows you completely—every action, every thought, every feeling, every detail. How does that make you feel? How does it feel to know that Jesus also understands you completely? How long will Jesus love you?

Your Anxious Thoughts

Worship Me only. Whatever occupies your mind the most becomes your god. Worries, if indulged, develop into idols. Anxiety gains a life of its own, parasitically infesting your mind. Break free from this bondage by affirming your trust in Me and refreshing yourself in My Presence. What goes on in your mind is invisible, undetectable to other people. But I read your thoughts continually, searching for evidence of trust in Me. I rejoice when your mind turns toward Me. Guard your thoughts diligently; good thought-choices will keep you close to Me.

READ TOGETHER

He will have no fear of bad news; his heart is steadfast, trusting in the Lord.

—Psalm 112:7

Read More: 1 Corinthians 13:11; Psalm 139:23–24 nasb

Don't Worship Your Worries

Worship your worries? That sounds crazy, doesn't it? But whatever you think about the most becomes your god, your idol, the thing you worship. When your worries take on a life of their own and take over your thoughts, you are worshiping your worries.

I want you to break free from your worries. How? By trusting Me. By thinking about Me. By worshiping only Me. No one else knows what goes on inside your mind—not your friends, not your teachers, not even your parents. But *I* know your every thought, so be careful concerning what you choose to think about. I am constantly searching your thoughts for a sign of your trust in Me. When I find that your thoughts are about Me, I rejoice! Choose to think about Me more and more; this will keep you close to Me.

TALK TOGETHER

Do worries ever seem to take over your thoughts? How might thinking about Jesus instead of your worries make a difference? How does thinking about Jesus instead of worrying about your problems help you trust in Him?

I NEVER CHANGE

IN A WORLD OF UNRELENTING CHANGES, I am the One who never changes. *I am the Alpha and the Omega, the First and the Last, the Beginning and the End.* Find in Me the stability for which you have yearned.

I created a beautifully ordered world: one that reflects My perfection. Now, however, the world is under the bondage of sin and evil. Every person on the planet faces gaping jaws of uncertainty. The only antidote to this poisonous threat is drawing closer to Me. In My Presence you can face uncertainty with perfect Peace.

READ TOGETHER

"I am the Alpha and the Omega, the First and the Last, the Beginning and the End."

—REVELATION 22:13

READ MORE: ROMANS 5:12; JOHN 16:33 AMP

Exactly the Same

In a world where everything changes—the weather, your friends, and sometimes even your family—I am the One who never changes. I am exactly the same as I was at the beginning of the world, and I will be exactly the same at the end of it. You can always count on Me.

I created a beautiful, perfect world for you. But sin came into the world, and since then the world is constantly changing. Nothing stays the same, and nothing is ever for certain—in this world. But remember that I have overcome the world. So stay close to Me. In My never-changing, always-loving Presence, you can face the changes of this world with peace—*My* Peace.

TALK TOGETHER

What are some things that change? Jesus never changes. How is that different from the way of the world? Why is it so important?

SET APART

TAKE TIME TO BE HOLY. The word *holy* does not mean *goody-goody*; it means *set apart for sacred use*. That is what these quiet moments in My Presence are accomplishing within you. As you focus your mind and heart on Me, you are being transformed: re-created into the one I designed you to be. This process requires blocks of time set aside for communion with Me.

The benefits of this practice are limitless. Emotional and physical healing are enhanced by your soaking in the Light of My Presence. You experience a nearness to Me that strengthens your faith and fills you with Peace. You open yourself up to receive the many blessings that I have prepared for you. You become a cleansed *temple of My Holy Spirit*, who is able to do in and through you *immeasurably more than you ask or imagine*. These are just some of the benefits of being still in My Presence.

READ TOGETHER

Do you not know that your body is a temple of the Holy Spirit, who is in you, whom you have received from God? You are not your own.

—1 CORINTHIANS 6:19

READ MORE: 2 THESSALONIANS 1:10;
PSALM 27:4; EPHESIANS 3:20

Time to Be Holy

Take time to be holy. But how? *Holy* doesn't mean being a goody-goody, or thinking you are better than others. Being holy simply means setting yourself apart for sacred use—*My* use.

Spend some quiet moments with Me. Let Me work in your heart and mind. I am re-creating you into the person I designed you to be.

Be sure to set aside enough time for just being with Me. Your closeness to Me will strengthen your faith and fill you with My Peace. It will also prepare you for the many blessings I want to give you.

When you take time to be holy, your heart becomes a clean temple of My Holy Spirit. He is able to do more in and through you than you could ever ask or imagine. So make time for Me. You won't regret it.

TALK TOGETHER

What does it mean "to be holy"? Does knowing that your body is a temple for the Holy Spirit change the way you think about yourself? What things can Jesus do through you when you take time to be holy?

LIGHT AND MOMENTARY TROUBLES

TRY TO SEE THINGS more and more from My perspective. Let the Light of My Presence so fully fill your mind that you view the world through Me. When little things don't go as you had hoped, look to Me lightheartedly and say, "Oh, well." This simple discipline can protect you from being burdened with an accumulation of petty cares and frustrations. If you practice this diligently, you will make a life-changing discovery: You realize that most of the things that worry you are not important. If you shrug them off immediately and return your focus to Me, you will walk through your days with lighter steps and a joyful heart.

When serious problems come your way, you will have more reserves for dealing with them. You will not have squandered your energy on petty problems. You may even reach the point where you can agree with the apostle Paul that all your troubles are *light and momentary* compared with *the eternal glory* being achieved by them.

READ TOGETHER

A man's steps are directed by the LORD. How then can anyone understand his own way?

—PROVERBS 20:24

READ MORE: PSALM 36:9 NKJV; 2 CORINTHIANS 4:17–18

Shake It Off

I have a perfect plan for your life. So trust Me and try to see things from My point of view. When things don't go quite the way you expected, shake them off. Look up at Me, shrug your shoulders, and say with a grin, "Oh, well." Then just let them go—and move on.

This simple act of trust will keep you from weighing yourself down with little frustrations. With enough practice, you will discover that most of the things you worry about just aren't that important. Your energy and time won't be wasted on things that really don't matter—and you'll have the strength to deal with big problems when they do come your way.

You know that thing that's bothering you right now? Shake it off, and let's move on together.

TALK TOGETHER

What do you usually do when things don't go the way you had planned? Are you able to "shake it off"? Does knowing that Jesus has a perfect plan for your life help you not to waste time worrying about little things?

Stay in Touch

I am calling you to a life of constant communion with Me. Basic training includes learning to live above your circumstances, even while interacting on that cluttered plane of life. You yearn for a simplified lifestyle so that your communication with Me can be uninterrupted. But I challenge you to relinquish the fantasy of an uncluttered world. Accept each day just as it comes, and find Me in the midst of it all.

Talk with Me about every aspect of your day, including your feelings. Remember that your ultimate goal is not to control or fix everything around you; it is to keep communing with Me. A successful day is one in which you have stayed in touch with Me, even if many things remain undone at the end of the day. Do not let your to-do list (written or mental) become an idol directing your life. Instead, ask My Spirit to guide you moment by moment. He will keep you close to Me.

READ TOGETHER

Pray continually.

—1 Thessalonians 5:17

Read More: Proverbs 3:6; Galatians 5:25

Yes, Everything

I am waiting to hear from you. Tell Me about every detail of your day. I want to know what happened at home and at school, and how you felt about it. The big stuff, the little stuff, even the crazy stuff that you just don't understand. I want to be that best Friend you just can't wait to talk to.

Remember, I don't expect you to do everything perfectly. What I do expect is that you will come to Me in prayer about everything— *yes, everything*—that happens in your life. The good stuff, the bad stuff, the stuff you would never tell anyone else.

A great day is not just one in which everything goes your way. A truly great day is one in which you stay in touch with Me. Talk to Me, and My Spirit will guide you every minute, every step of the way.

TALK TOGETHER

How often do you talk to your parents or your friends? Do you tell them about the details of your day? What does Jesus want you to talk to Him about? Is there anything that you shouldn't tell Jesus?

On the Palms of My Hands

Nothing can separate you from My Love. Let this divine assurance trickle through your mind and into your heart and soul. Whenever you start to feel fearful or anxious, repeat this unconditional promise: "Nothing can separate me from Your Love, Jesus."

Most of mankind's misery stems from feeling unloved. In the midst of adverse circumstances, people tend to feel that love has been withdrawn and they have been forsaken. This feeling of abandonment is often worse than the adversity itself. Be assured that I never abandon any of My children, not even temporarily. *I will never leave you or forsake you!* My Presence watches over you continually. *I have engraved you on the palms of My hands.*

READ TOGETHER

"No one will be able to stand up against you all the days of your life. As I was with Moses, so I will be with you; I will never leave you nor forsake you."

—Joshua 1:5

Read More: Romans 8:38–39; Isaiah 49:15–16

I Will Never Leave You

Nothing can separate you from My Love. *Nothing.* Not bullies, not tough times, not even Satan himself. I will never leave you.

Most of the misery in this world comes from feeling lonely and unloved. Especially when times are tough, people often feel that I have left them all alone. And that feeling can be even worse than the problems they are facing. But know this: I never leave you—not even for a second. I am constantly watching over you. If you feel alone or frightened, ask Me to comfort you with My Presence. Then repeat these promises to yourself: "Nothing can separate me from Your Love, Jesus. . . . You will never leave me."

TALK TOGETHER

Think about those two promises—nothing can separate you from Jesus' love and Jesus will never leave you. What do these promises tell you about how Jesus feels about you? How can these promises help you when times are tough?

A Time for Everything

STOP TRYING TO WORK THINGS OUT before their times have come. Accept the limitations of living one day at a time. When something comes to your attention, ask Me whether or not it is part of today's agenda. If it isn't, release it into My care and go on about today's duties. When you follow this practice, there will be a beautiful simplicity about your life: *a time for everything, and everything in its time.*

A life lived close to Me is not complicated or cluttered. When your focus is on My Presence, many things that once troubled you lose their power over you. Though the world around you is messy and confusing, remember that *I have overcome the world. I have told you these things, so that in Me you may have Peace.*

READ TOGETHER

There is a time for everything, and a season for every activity under heaven.

—ECCLESIASTES 3:1

READ MORE: ECCLESIASTES 8:6–7; JOHN 16:33

Everything in Its Own Time

Stop trying to work things out before their time has come. You can't take Friday's math test on Thursday. You can't celebrate your August birthday in June. And you can't make My will happen before the right time.

Accept that you must live one day at a time. When something pops into your mind, take a moment to ask Me whether it's part of My plan for you today—or not. If it isn't, trust Me to take care of it. Then forget about it, and concentrate on what you need to do *today*.

Your life will be much less complicated and confusing. There is a time for everything—and I will help you do everything I want you to do, in its own time.

TALK TOGETHER

Do you wish today was your birthday? Can you make that happen? Even though you know that Jesus' timing is perfect, you can't change things, and it can still be difficult to wait. What can you do when you feel impatient?

My Goodness

TASTE AND SEE THAT I AM GOOD. This command contains an invitation to experience My living Presence. It also contains a promise. The more you experience Me, the more convinced you become of My goodness. This knowledge is essential to your faith-walk. When adversities strike, the human instinct is to doubt My goodness. My ways are mysterious, even to those who know Me intimately. *As the heavens are higher than the earth, so are My ways and thoughts higher than your ways and thoughts.* Do not try to fathom My ways. Instead, spend time enjoying Me and experiencing My goodness.

READ TOGETHER

Taste and see that the LORD is good; blessed is the man who takes refuge in him.

—PSALM 34:8

READ MORE: ISAIAH 55:8–9; PSALM 100:5 NKJV

I Am Good

I *am* good. Walk with Me today and see that for yourself. The more time you spend with Me, the more you will see just how good I am. And I promise to do only what is good for you.

When hard times come, many people start to doubt My goodness. But troubles are just part of living in this imperfect world. And I can use your troubles to grow your faith.

I know that doesn't always make sense to you. You won't always understand the "why" of things. I am God, and My thoughts and My ways are incredibly bigger and more complicated than yours. When you don't understand, just *trust* that I am good—and that I *always* work for good in your life.

TALK TOGETHER

What does it mean to say that God is good? When is it easiest to see God's goodness? When is it hardest? How do you see God's goodness even in the hardest of times?

ONE STEP AT A TIME

WALK PEACEFULLY WITH ME through this day. You are wondering how you will cope with all that is expected of you. You must traverse this day like any other: one step at a time. Instead of mentally rehearsing how you will do this or that, keep your mind on My Presence and on taking the next step. The more demanding your day, the more help you can expect from Me. This is a training opportunity since I designed you for deep dependence on your Shepherd-King. Challenging times wake you up and amplify your awareness of needing My help.

When you don't know what to do, wait while I open the way before you. Trust that I know what I'm doing, and be ready to follow My lead. *I will give strength to you, and I will bless you with Peace.*

READ TOGETHER

The LORD gives strength to his people; the LORD blesses his people with peace.

—PSALM 29:11

READ MORE: EXODUS 33:14;
DEUTERONOMY 33:25; HEBREWS 13:20–21

Challenges Are Actually Chances

Walk peacefully with Me through this day. You are wondering how you will handle all the things you need to do. But there's really only one way to go through this day—or any day: one step at a time.

I see you rehearsing how you will do this or that—as if you were getting ready for a play. Don't waste time rehearsing; turn to Me instead. Ask Me to guide you, and I will.

One of the greatest things about walking with Me is that the tougher your day is, the more of My Power you can see. The harder things get, the more I help. See your challenges as chances—chances to depend on Me more than usual.

When you don't know what to do, wait for Me. You can be sure that *I* know what I'm doing. So be ready to follow My lead. As we face this day together, I will give strength to you and bless you with My Peace.

TALK TOGETHER

When you feel overwhelmed by what you need to do, do you dive in anyway? Or do you ask Jesus to show you what really needs to be done? How might talking with Jesus take away that "overwhelmed" feeling?

Your Need for Me

You need Me every moment. Your awareness of your constant need for Me is your greatest strength. Your neediness, properly handled, is a link to My Presence. However, there are pitfalls that you must be on guard against: self-pity, self-preoccupation, giving up. Your inadequacy presents you with a continual choice—deep dependence on Me or despair. The emptiness you feel within will be filled either with problems or with My Presence. Make Me central in your consciousness by *praying continually*: simple, short prayers flowing out of the present moment. Use My Name liberally, to remind you of My Presence. *Keep on asking and you will receive, so that your gladness may be full and complete.*

READ TOGETHER

"Up to this time you have not asked a [single] thing in My Name [as presenting all that *I am*]; but now ask and keep on asking and you will receive, so that your joy (gladness, delight) may be full and complete."

—John 16:24 AMP

Read More: Psalm 86:7; 1 Thessalonians 5:17

The Empty Spot

I created you with a need. It is an empty spot inside you. You may try to fill that empty spot with stuff or with friends, or even with sin. It may even work for a short while. But sooner or later, those things will fail you and you will be left feeling even emptier than before. I am the only one who can fill your empty spot.

You need Me every second of every day. And you can reach Me every second of every day. Pray all the time. It doesn't have to be a long prayer or one full of fancy words. Just say a simple, short prayer about whatever is happening at the moment. Let Me know you are thinking about Me. Or simply say My Name. Or whisper to yourself a verse from My Word. Just keep talking to Me; I will always be listening.

TALK TOGETHER

First Thessalonians 5:17 says, "Never stop praying" (ICB). How do you pray? Is there only one way to pray—with head bowed and eyes closed? How is it possible to never stop praying?

WHO DEFINES YOU?

BEWARE OF SEEING YOURSELF through other people's eyes. There are several dangers to this practice. First of all, it is nearly impossible to discern what others actually think of you. Moreover, their views of you are variable: subject to each viewer's spiritual, emotional, and physical condition. The major problem with letting others define you is that it borders on idolatry. Your concern to please others dampens your desire to please Me, your Creator.

It is much more real to see yourself through *My eyes*. My gaze upon you is steady and sure, untainted by sin. Through My eyes you can see yourself as one who is deeply, eternally loved. Rest in My loving gaze, and you will receive deep Peace. Respond to My loving Presence by *worshiping Me in spirit and in truth*.

READ TOGETHER

And without faith it is impossible to please God, because anyone who comes to him must believe that he exists and that he rewards those who earnestly seek him.

—HEBREWS 11:6

READ MORE: ROMANS 5:5; JOHN 4:23–24

People-Pleasers

Don't be a people-pleaser. People-pleasers let their lives be ruled by what other people think. *I have to wear these clothes so they'll hang out with me. I can't sit with those kids—everyone will think I'm a loser. I don't want to try that stuff, but if I don't, I won't fit in.*

You can end up in scary or even dangerous situations trying to please others. Other people aren't perfect. They don't have perfect judgment, and they don't always want what is best for you. Besides, you can't really know what they truly think of you. So being a people-pleaser is foolish.

Live to please Me instead. Only I am perfect and only I care about you perfectly. Don't look at yourself through the eyes of other people, or treat their opinions as being more important than Mine. See yourself through *My* eyes—and you will see a child of God who is deeply and perfectly loved.

TALK TOGETHER

Have you ever done something to make people like you, even if you knew that what you did was wrong? Did it make everyone like you? God tells us not to try to please people. Who does He want us to try to please in the way we live?

My Perfect Love

Let My Love seep into the inner recesses of your being. Do not close off any part of yourself from Me. I know you inside and out, so do not try to present a "cleaned-up" self to Me. Wounds that you shut away from the Light of My Love will fester and become wormy. Secret sins that you "hide" from Me can split off and develop lives of their own, controlling you without your realizing it.

Open yourself fully to My transforming Presence. Let My brilliant Love-Light search out and destroy hidden fears. This process requires time alone with Me, as My Love soaks into your innermost being. Enjoy *My perfect Love, which expels every trace of fear.*

READ TOGETHER

There is no fear in love [dread does not exist], but full-grown (complete, perfect) love turns fear out of doors and expels every trace of terror! For fear brings with it the thought of punishment, and [so] he who is afraid has not reached the full maturity of love [is not yet grown into love's complete perfection].

—1 John 4:18 AMP

Read More: Psalm 139:1–4, 23–24

Soak in My Love

Shut your eyes and imagine you are standing outside in a warm summer rain. The raindrops drench you, soaking you through and through. Let My Love do the same for you. Let it soak through you and wash away hidden fears.

There is no point in trying to hide *anything* from Me. I already know everything about you—and I *still* love you. When you try to hide away parts of yourself, it only hurts you more. Hurts and disappointments can become infected with anger and bitterness. Secret sins can take on a life of their own, controlling you before you even realize it.

Don't close off pieces of yourself from Me. Invite Me in. Show Me all those dark thoughts and feelings. As you spend time with Me, the Light of My Love will chase them away. Rest in My perfect Love—it drives out every fear.

TALK TOGETHER

Are there secrets, fears, or sins that you try to hide from God? Share those secrets with Him—He knows anyway and they won't change His love for you. How might telling God everything chase away your fears?

THE PATH OF MY CHOOSING

YOU ARE ON THE PATH of My choosing. There is no randomness about your life. Here and Now comprise the coordinates of your daily life. Most people let their moments slip through their fingers, half-lived. They avoid the present by worrying about the future or longing for a better time and place. They forget that they are creatures who are subject to the limitations of time and space. They forget their Creator, who walks with them only in the present.

Every moment is alive with My glorious Presence, to those whose hearts are intimately connected with Mine. As you give yourself more and more to a life of constant communion with Me, you will find that you simply have no time for worry. Thus, you are freed to let My Spirit direct your steps, enabling you to walk along *the path of Peace.*

READ TOGETHER

To shine on those living in darkness and in the shadow of death, to guide our feet into the path of peace.

—LUKE 1:79

READ MORE: LUKE 12:25–26; JUDE VV. 24–25

Here-and-Now

I have lovingly created a path for your life. Nothing is by accident. Every twist, every turn, is a part of My plan.

Don't try to see what is up ahead on your path. And don't keep turning around and looking at the past. *Here-and-Now* is the only place you can live. When you are constantly looking at the past or the future, today slips through your fingers, half-lived. Don't worry about the test you blew last week. Don't worry about whether or not you'll get invited to that party next week. Letting go of past and future worries frees you up to enjoy the Here-and-Now.

Today is the day that is filled with My glorious Presence. Today is the day I have filled with blessings. Today is the day I give you My Peace.

TALK TOGETHER

Can you think of something that you thought was going to be bad in your life and it turned out being good? Do you sometimes worry about what might happen? Then how often do the bad things you worry about really happen? Hardly ever! That's why God says to trust Him one day at a time.

Content in All Circumstances

Rejoice in Me always! No matter what is going on, you can rejoice in your Love-relationship with Me. This is *the secret of being content in all circumstances.* So many people dream of the day when they will finally be happy: when they are out of debt, when their children are out of trouble, when they have more leisure time, and so on. While they daydream, their moments are trickling into the ground like precious balm spilling wastefully from overturned bottles.

Fantasizing about future happiness will never bring fulfillment because fantasy is unreality. Even though I am invisible, I am far more Real than the world you see around you. My reality is eternal and unchanging. Bring your moments to Me, and I will fill them with vibrant Joy. *Now* is the time to rejoice in My Presence!

READ TOGETHER

Rejoice in the Lord always. I will say it again: Rejoice! . . . I know what it is to be in need, and I know what it is to have plenty. I have learned the secret of being content in any and every situation, whether well fed or hungry, whether living in plenty or in want.

—Philippians 4:4, 12

READ MORE: Psalm 102:27; 1 Peter 1:8

The Secret of Being Happy

Choose to be happy in Me—no matter what is going on around you.

Don't wait for everything in your life to be perfect before you decide to be happy. Too many people waste their lives dreaming about the time when they'll finally be happy—when they are out of school, when they can drive, when they have their own job or house, and so on. But while they are daydreaming, life is passing them by. Life is *today*, not "when . . ."

If your life is going great, be happy and enjoy My blessings. If times are tough, be happy because you know these problems will go away. And don't forget this either: You have the promise of a problem-free life in heaven—*forever*—with Me!

Don't wait to be happy. Come to Me and I will show you how to be happy *today*.

TALK TOGETHER

What does it mean to be happy? Does it have to mean that everything is going your way? How can you still be happy when nothing seems to be going your way?

Seek Me and Find Me

Seek My Face, and you will find more than you ever dreamed possible. *Let Me displace worry at the center of your being.* I am like a supersaturated cloud, showering Peace into the pool of your mind. My Nature is to bless. Your nature is to receive with thanksgiving. This is a true fit, designed before the foundation of the world. Glorify Me by receiving My blessings gratefully.

I am the goal of all your searching. *When you seek Me, you find Me* and are satisfied. When lesser goals capture your attention, I fade into the background of your life. I am still there, watching and waiting, but you function as if you were alone. Actually, My Light shines on every situation you will ever face. Live radiantly by expanding your focus to include Me in all your moments. Let nothing dampen your search for Me.

READ TOGETHER

When You said, "Seek My face," my heart said to You, "Your face, Lord, I will seek."

—Psalm 27:8 nkjv

Read More: Philippians 4:7 the message; Jeremiah 29:13

I Am Still Here

When you seek Me, You will find more than you ever dreamed possible. I will replace your worries with peace, and I will shower you with blessings.

I am all that you are searching and hoping for. That empty place inside you? The one you've tried to fill with stuff, and friends, and so many other things? I am the only One who can fill it. Seek Me!

All the stuff and busyness of this world may sometimes distract you and take your attention away from Me. But I am watching and waiting for you to return to Me. And when you do search for Me again, you will find that I am still here with you—right where I have always been.

TALK TOGETHER

What are some things you have searched for? Did you find them? Read Jeremiah 29:13. How should you search for Jesus? Do you believe you will always find Him? Why?

UNIQUELY RIGHT FOR YOU

I AM LEADING YOU along a way that is uniquely right for you. The closer to Me you grow, the more fully you become your true self—the one I designed you to be. Because you are one of a kind, the path you are traveling with Me diverges increasingly from that of other people. However, in My mysterious wisdom and ways, I enable you to follow this solitary path while staying in close contact with others. In fact, the more completely you devote yourself to Me, the more freely you can love people.

Marvel at the beauty of a life intertwined with My Presence. Rejoice as we journey together in intimate communion. Enjoy the adventure of finding yourself through losing yourself in Me.

READ TOGETHER

Dear friends, let us love one another, for love comes from God. Everyone who loves has been born of God and knows God. Whoever does not love does not know God, because God is love.

—1 JOHN 4:7–8

READ MORE: 2 CORINTHIANS 5:17;
EPHESIANS 2:10; JOHN 15:4

One of a Kind

You are one of a kind. There is no one else like you. That is why I created a path just for you. As you go with Me down your path, you become more and more the person I designed you to be.

Because you are one of a kind, the path you are traveling along is not the same as the paths of others. They are following the paths that I created just for them.

However, in My own mysterious ways, I have made you able to follow your own path while also staying in close contact with others. In fact, the more you stay in step with Me—because you love Me—the more freely you can love other people.

Be amazed at how wonderfully I work in your life. The more you follow My path for you, the more you become who you really are. And the more you love Me, the more you can love others.

TALK TOGETHER

Jesus created you with unique, special skills and talents—just as He gave every person unique gifts. What does that tell you about the path your life is taking versus the paths of others? How can loving Jesus more help you love others more?

A Better Way to Live This Day

Let Me help you get through this day. There are many possible paths to travel between your getting up in the morning and your lying down at night. Stay alert to the many choice-points along the way, being continually aware of My Presence. You will get through this day one way or the other. One way is to moan and groan, stumbling along with shuffling feet. This will get you to the end of the day eventually, but there is a better way. You can choose to walk with Me along the path of Peace, leaning on Me as much as you need. There will still be difficulties along the way, but you can face them confidently in My strength. Thank Me for each problem you encounter, and watch to see how I transform trials into blessings.

READ TOGETHER

And do not grumble, as some of them did—and were killed by the destroying angel.

—1 Corinthians 10:10

Read More: Luke 1:79; 2 Samuel 22:29–30

A Day That Is Just Right

When you get up in the morning, you get to decide what kind of day you will have. I don't mean that you can decide you are going to have a completely problem-free day, a Saturday, or even a snow day. I mean that you choose how you will view this day. And there are really only two choices: to complain about everything you don't like, or to stay close to Me—so you can see things *My* way.

You can choose to see the rain, or the rainbow. You can choose to see a mountain of homework, or the chance to learn something new. You can resent your parents for not letting you go to that movie, or you can be grateful that someone cares enough to say no sometimes.

You can choose to see everything that is wrong, or you can choose to see Me. If you choose Me, I'll show you how all those wrongs can turn into a day that is just right.

TALK TOGETHER

Read Philippians 4:8. Can the things you choose to think about affect how you feel about your day? When you choose to keep Jesus in your thoughts, how does that change your thoughts and your day? Will you choose to grumble at problems or to see the blessings Jesus gives you each day?

My Unfailing Love

I LOVE YOU regardless of how well you are performing. Sometimes you feel uneasy, wondering if you are doing enough to be worthy of My Love. No matter how exemplary your behavior, the answer to that question will always be no. Your performance and My Love are totally different issues, which you need to sort out. *I love you with an everlasting Love* that flows out from eternity without limits or conditions. *I have clothed you in My robe of righteousness*, and this is an eternal transaction: Nothing and no one can reverse it. Therefore, your accomplishment as a Christian has no bearing on My Love for you. Even your ability to assess how well you are doing on a given day is flawed. Your limited human perspective and the condition of your body, with its mercurial variations, distort your evaluations.

Bring your performance anxiety to Me, and receive in its place *My unfailing Love.* Try to stay conscious of My loving Presence with you in all that you do, and I will direct your steps.

READ TOGETHER

Let your face shine on your servant; save me in your unfailing love.
—PSALM 31:16

READ MORE: JEREMIAH 31:3; ISAIAH 61:10; PSALM 107:8

No Matter What

Do you know that uneasy, twisty feeling you get in the pit of your stomach when you have to give a speech? Or you're up at bat? Or you're next in the dance recital? You worry if you'll be good enough, and if people will like your performance.

Sometimes you can even get that uneasy, twisty feeling about Me. You wonder if you are doing enough to be worthy of My Love. Well, the answer is no. It doesn't matter how great you act or how many things you do to serve Me, you can never be *worthy* of My Love. No one can. But that's the greatest thing about My Love—you don't *have* to be worthy. It's a gift—free and clear. You don't have to earn it. You just have to accept it.

So relax. Do the best you can. And know that I will love you—no matter what!

TALK TOGETHER

When did you feel uncomfortable that you weren't going to be good enough to do something? Have you ever felt like you were not good enough for Jesus to love you? Do you know that Jesus has never had that thought about you? You don't have to be smart or pretty or perfect at anything. You just have to accept His gift of love for you!

I Bring Good Out of Problems

Make friends with the problems in your life. Though many things feel random and wrong, remember that I am sovereign over everything. *I can fit everything into a pattern for good,* but only to the extent that you trust Me. Every problem can teach you something, transforming you little by little into the masterpiece I created you to be. The very same problem can become a stumbling block over which you fall if you react with distrust and defiance. The choice is up to you, and you will have to choose many times each day whether to trust Me or defy Me.

The best way to befriend your problems is to thank Me for them. This simple act opens your mind to the possibility of benefits flowing from your difficulties. You can even give persistent problems nicknames, helping you to approach them with familiarity rather than with dread. The next step is to introduce them to Me, enabling Me to embrace them in My loving Presence. I will not necessarily remove your problems, but My wisdom is sufficient to bring good out of every one of them.

READ TOGETHER

We are assured and know that [God being a partner in their labor] all things work together and are [fitting into a plan] for good to and for those who love God and are called according to [His] design and purpose.

—Romans 8:28 amp

Read More: 1 Corinthians 1:23–24

Make Friends with Your Problems

Make friends with the problems in your life. Yes, that's right. And don't forget to thank Me for them either. That sounds crazy, doesn't it? But I can use every single problem to teach you something. Just as a sculptor chisels away bits of rough stone to reveal a beautiful masterpiece, I can use your problems to chip away rough bits of stubbornness, pride, and selfishness, to reveal My masterpiece—you!

It's your choice. You can keep your problems all to yourself, so that they grow and become stumbling blocks that trip you up. *Or* you can make friends with your problems by introducing them to Me and letting Me make them part of My plan. I may not take your problems away, but I will make something good come out of them.

TALK TOGETHER

How can your problems become your friends? What does it mean to "introduce" your problems to Jesus? What good thing can come out of your problems?

EVENING, MORNING, AND NOON

I AM THE GOD OF ALL TIME and all that is. Seek Me not only in morning quietness but consistently throughout the day. Do not let unexpected problems distract you from My Presence. Instead, talk with Me about everything, and watch confidently to see what I will do.

Adversity need not interrupt your communion with Me. When things go "wrong," you tend to react as if you're being punished. Instead of this negative response, try to view difficulties as blessings in disguise. *Make Me your Refuge by pouring out your heart to Me, trusting in Me at all times.*

READ TOGETHER

Evening, morning and noon I cry out in distress, and he hears my voice.

—PSALM 55:17

READ MORE: PSALM 105:3 NKJV; PSALM 32:6; PSALM 62:8

The Position of Your Heart

I am the God of all time and of all that is. And I am waiting to hear from you—morning, noon, and night.

Don't just pray to Me in the quiet of the morning. Don't just pray to Me at church or when things are going well. And don't just pray to Me with your head bowed and your eyes closed. Talk to Me every day, at any time, in any place and situation—in class, on the soccer field, while practicing piano or doing homework or texting your friends. Pray when you're in trouble and when you're happy. Time with Me is what matters, not what time it is.

You can talk to Me lying down, sitting up, or with arms stretched up to heaven. Your eyes can be opened or closed. I don't care about the position of your body—I care about the position of your heart. And when your heart is seeking Me, I will hear you.

TALK TOGETHER

When do you pray? Do you pray only at certain times or in certain ways? Is *how* or *where* or *what time* you pray important? How is the position of your heart more important than the position of your body?

WHEN YOU NEED COMFORT

LOOK TO ME CONTINUALLY for help, comfort, and companionship. Because I am always by your side, the briefest glance can connect you with Me. When you look to Me for help, it flows freely from My Presence. This recognition of your need for Me, in small matters as well as in large ones, keeps you spiritually alive.

When you need comfort, I love to enfold you in My arms. I enable you not only to feel comforted but also to be a channel through whom I comfort others. Thus you are doubly blessed, because a living channel absorbs some of whatever flows through it.

My constant Companionship is the *pièce de résistance*: the summit of salvation blessings. No matter what losses you experience in your life, no one can take away this glorious gift.

READ TOGETHER

Praise be to the God and Father of our Lord Jesus Christ, the Father of compassion and the God of all comfort, who comforts us in all our troubles, so that we can comfort those in any trouble with the comfort we ourselves have received from God.

—2 CORINTHIANS 1:3–4

READ MORE: PSALM 34:4–6; PSALM 105:4

I Am Your Comfort

This world is tough. Some days your spirit can really take a beating. Some days you just need to be comforted.

Because I am always with you, it takes only the slightest glance in My direction—the softest whisper—to connect you with Me and My comfort. I wrap you up in My arms so that you are protected from the kicks and punches of this world.

I comfort you, and then I bless you with the ability to comfort others. You see, I am the God who can bring good out of all things. Out of your hurts, I give you understanding—an understanding of how others are hurting—and an ability to comfort them.

TALK TOGETHER

Do you have to yell for Jesus to hear you? What do you need to do for Jesus to hear you? How can Jesus' comfort feel like a wonderful, warm hug?

DON'T JUDGE

MY CHILDREN make a pastime of judging one another—and themselves. But I am the only capable Judge, and I have acquitted you through My own blood. Your acquittal came at the price of My unparalleled sacrifice. That is why I am highly offended when I hear My children judge one another or indulge in self-hatred.

If you live close to Me and absorb My Word, the Holy Spirit will guide and correct you as needed. There is *no condemnation* for those who belong to Me.

READ TOGETHER

"Do not judge, and you will not be judged. Do not condemn, and you will not be condemned. Forgive, and you will be forgiven."

—LUKE 6:37

READ MORE: 2 TIMOTHY 4:8; TITUS 3:5; ROMANS 8:1

Not Guilty

My children make a hobby out of judging one another—and themselves. But *I* am the only true Judge. I hate seeing My children put themselves down or judge others. This is not My way for you.

I gave you the ability to choose what is right. If you live close to Me and follow My teaching, the Spirit will guide you and correct you. I died on the cross so that you would be washed clean of all your sins. I gave My own blood so that you would be fully forgiven.

So forgive others, and forgive yourself. Let My Spirit help you make good choices and correct you when you need it. And always remember, I do not condemn My children.

TALK TOGETHER

What is the difference between judging a person and judging between what is right and wrong? We forgive because Christ forgave us. Why is it sometimes difficult to forgive? When might you need to forgive yourself?

Seek My Face

Seek My Face more and more. You are really just beginning your journey of intimacy with Me. It is not an easy road, but it is a delightful and privileged way: a treasure hunt. I am the Treasure, and the Glory of My Presence glistens and shimmers along the way. Hardships are part of the journey too. I mete them out ever so carefully, in just the right dosage, with a tenderness you can hardly imagine. Do not recoil from afflictions since they are among My most favored gifts. *Trust Me and don't be afraid, for I am your Strength and Song.*

READ TOGETHER

Surely God is my salvation; I will trust and not be afraid. The LORD, the LORD, is my strength and my song; he has become my salvation.

—ISAIAH 12:2

READ MORE: PSALM 27:8 NKJV; 2 CORINTHIANS 4:7–8

The Treasure Hunt

Did you know that you are on a treasure hunt? It's not a hunt for a prize, a bag of candy, or even a pirate's chest full of gold. It's a hunt for Me. I am the Treasure. I've given you the map of My Holy Word to follow, and I've given you My Spirit to guide you.

The road you must take is not an easy one, but the Treasure is worth it! All along the way, I'm waiting to give you jewels of blessings. Hardships are part of the journey too—just as they are with any great adventure. But don't be afraid; I'm with you. I will give you strength, and I will fill your heart with a joy that will make you sing. And at the end of your journey is the greatest treasure of all—eternity with Me!

TALK TOGETHER

Is Jesus your greatest treasure? If others looked at your life, would they see that He is your greatest treasure? Would they see you using His Word as your map through life?

I Live in You

I AM *CHRIST IN YOU, the hope of Glory*. The One who walks beside you, holding you by your hand, is the same One who lives within you. This is a deep, unfathomable mystery. You and I are intertwined in an intimacy involving every fiber of your being. The Light of My Presence shines within you, as well as upon you. I am in you, and you are in Me; therefore nothing in heaven or on earth can separate you from Me!

As you sit quietly in My Presence, your awareness of My Life within you is heightened. This produces the *Joy of the Lord, which is your strength. I, the God of hope, fill you with all Joy and Peace as you trust in Me, so that you may bubble over with hope by the power of the Holy Spirit.*

READ TOGETHER

May the God of your hope so fill you with all joy and peace in believing [through the experience of your faith] that by the power of the Holy Spirit you may abound and be overflowing (bubbling over) with hope.

—ROMANS 15:13 AMP

READ MORE: COLOSSIANS 1:27; ISAIAH 42:6; NEHEMIAH 8:10

Enjoy the Mysteries

With Me, some things are a mystery: I am the One who walks beside you, holding your hand—*and* I am the One who lives in you to comfort and guide you. I am able to be *both*, all at the same time.

Here's another mystery: Not only am I in you, but you are also *in Me*. We are woven together like the threads of a cloth. There is nothing in heaven or on earth that can separate you from Me!

As you think about these amazing mysteries, be happy that you have a God who loves you so very much. Let the knowledge of My Presence in you and around you fill you up with My Joy and Peace. These are mysteries that you can't understand—but you *can* enjoy them!

TALK TOGETHER

There are many things about God that are a mystery. One of the greatest is that He is both *in* you and *with* you. What does God's constant, never-ending Presence mean for your life? Does it make you more confident and more willing to tell others about Him?

Your Best Friend

I am your best Friend, as well as your King. Walk hand in hand with Me through your life. Together we will face whatever each day brings: pleasures, hardships, adventures, disappointments. Nothing is wasted when it is shared with Me. *I can bring beauty out of the ashes* of lost dreams. I can glean Joy out of sorrow, Peace out of adversity. Only a Friend who is also the King of kings could accomplish this divine alchemy. There is no other like Me!

The friendship I offer you is practical and down-to-earth, yet it is saturated with heavenly Glory. Living in My Presence means living in two realms simultaneously: the visible world and unseen, eternal reality. I have equipped you to stay conscious of Me while walking along dusty, earthbound paths.

READ TOGETHER

"Greater love has no one than this, that he lay down his life for his friends. You are my friends if you do what I command. I no longer call you servants, because a servant does not know his master's business. Instead, I have called you friends, for everything that I learned from my Father I have made known to you."

—John 15:13–15

READ MORE: Isaiah 61:3; 2 Corinthians 6:10

No Other Friend Like Me

I am your best Friend, *and* I am your King.

My friendship is practical and down-to-earth. As your Friend, I am always here to listen and to help. Together we will face whatever each day brings: pleasures, hardships, adventures, disappointments.

But as your heavenly King, our friendship opens up so many more possibilities. As King, I can create something wonderful out of the ashes of lost dreams, Joy out of sorrow, and Peace out of problems.

And it's all because I love you. My Love for you is so great that I gave up heaven to come to earth as a helpless baby. It is so great that I lived in the dust and sin of this world. And it is so great that I died on the cross to save your soul. There is no other friend like Me!

TALK TOGETHER

What makes a good friend? What makes Jesus your very best Friend? Are there things you can do to be a better friend—not only to the people in your life but also to Jesus?

IMMEASURABLY MORE

I AM ABLE to do far beyond all that you ask or imagine. Come to Me with positive expectations, knowing that there is no limit to what I can accomplish. Ask My Spirit to control your mind so that you can think great thoughts of Me. Do not be discouraged by the fact that many of your prayers are yet unanswered. Time is a trainer, teaching you to wait upon Me, to trust Me in the dark. The more extreme your circumstances, the more likely you are to see *My Power and Glory* at work in the situation. Instead of letting difficulties draw you into worrying, try to view them as setting the scene for My glorious intervention. Keep your eyes and your mind wide open to all that I am doing in your life.

READ TOGETHER

Now to him who is able to do immeasurably more than all we ask or imagine, according to his power that is at work within us, to him be glory in the church and in Christ Jesus throughout all generations, for ever and ever! Amen.

—EPHESIANS 3:20–21

READ MORE: ROMANS 8:6;
ISAIAH 40:30–31 NKJV; REVELATION 5:13

Dare to Dream My Dream

Dream your biggest, most incredible dream—and then know that I am able to do far more than that, far more than you could ever ask or imagine. Allow Me to fill your mind with *My* dreams for you.

Don't be discouraged if your prayers are not answered right away. Time is a great teacher. It teaches you to be patient and to trust in My perfect plan—even when you don't know what is going to happen next.

When everything seems way too hard, that is when you can truly see My Power at work in your life. Don't let this world's craziness drag you into worry. Instead, choose to see all that I am doing around you. Remember, there is no limit to what I can do.

TALK TOGETHER

What is your biggest dream? How can you find out what Jesus' dream is for you? How does reading the Bible and praying help you know Jesus' plan for your life?

Worship Me

Meet Me in morning stillness, while the earth is fresh with the dew of My Presence. *Worship Me in the beauty of holiness.* Sing love songs to My holy Name. As you give yourself to Me, My Spirit swells within you till you are flooded with divine Presence.

The world's way of pursuing riches is grasping and hoarding. You attain *My* riches by letting go and giving. The more you give yourself to Me and My ways, the more I fill you with *inexpressible, heavenly Joy.*

READ TOGETHER

Give unto the Lord the glory due to His name; worship the Lord in the beauty of holiness.

—Psalm 29:2 nkjv

Read More: Psalm 9:10; 1 Peter 1:8

I Will Fill Your Life with Riches

Worship Me, and I will fill your life with glorious riches.

The world tells you that riches are money, cars, designer clothes, and beautiful jewelry. The world says grab them and hold on tight; store up these treasures for yourself.

But My riches are the far better treasures of Joy, Love, and Peace. And instead of storing them up only for yourself, I want you to share them. When you share My riches, they multiply—so that you and those around you are richer than ever before.

How can you get My riches? Worship Me! Come to Me in the quietness of morning. Praise Me for the beauty of a new day. Sing to Me of My holiness. Open your heart to Me, and let Me flood your soul with My riches.

TALK TOGETHER

What is worship? How can worship fill your life with riches? Read Matthew 6:19–21. How are the riches of Joy, Love, and Peace greater than the riches of the world?

Uncluttered

Do not be weighed down by the clutter in your life: lots of little chores to do sometime, in no particular order. If you focus too much on these petty tasks, trying to get them all out of the way, you will discover that they are endless. They can eat up as much time as you devote to them.

Instead of trying to do all your chores at once, choose the ones that need to be done today. Let the rest slip into the background of your mind so I can be in the forefront of your awareness. Remember that your ultimate goal is living close to Me, being responsive to My initiatives. I can communicate with you most readily when your mind is uncluttered and turned toward Me. Seek My Face continually throughout this day. Let My Presence bring order to your thoughts, infusing Peace into your entire being.

READ TOGETHER

"But seek first his kingdom and his righteousness, and all these things will be given to you as well."

—Matthew 6:33

Read More: Proverbs 16:3;
Psalm 27:8 nkjv; Isaiah 26:3 nkjv

Clearing the Clutter

Do not be overwhelmed by the clutter in your life. By "clutter," I'm not just talking about all that stuff under your bed. I'm including all those endless little chores that you need to do sometime, but not necessarily *now*. For instance, you told your friend you would download that song for her. And your bike tires really need airing up.

All those little tasks will eat up as much time as you give them. So, instead of trying to do everything at once, choose the chores that really need to be done today. Then let the rest of them slip to the back of your mind, so that *I* can be in the front of it.

Remember, your real goal in this life is not to check everything off a to-do list. It is to live close to Me. Seek My Face all throughout this day. Let My Presence clear away the clutter in your mind, and flood you with My Peace.

TALK TOGETHER

What sort of "clutter" fills up your thoughts and your days? Do you have time for Jesus? How can Jesus help you decide what is truly important and what is just "clutter"?

A Cheerful Heart

LEARN TO LAUGH at yourself more freely. Don't take yourself or your circumstances so seriously. Relax and know that I am *God with you*. When you desire My will above all else, life becomes much less threatening. Stop trying to monitor My responsibilities—things that are beyond your control. Find freedom by accepting the boundaries of your domain.

Laughter lightens your load and lifts your heart into heavenly places. Your laughter rises to heaven and blends with angelic melodies of praise. Just as parents delight in the laughter of their children, so I delight in hearing My children laugh. I rejoice when you trust Me enough to enjoy your life lightheartedly.

Do not miss the Joy of My Presence by carrying the weight of the world on your shoulders. Rather, *take My yoke upon you and learn from Me. My yoke is comfortable and pleasant; My burden is light and easily borne.*

READ TOGETHER

She is clothed with strength and dignity; she can laugh at the days to come.

—PROVERBS 31:25

READ MORE: PROVERBS 17:22;
MATTHEW 1:23; MATTHEW 11:29–30 AMP

Laughing at Troubles

Learn to laugh at yourself and at the world. Instead of getting bogged down in the mud of worry and fear, laugh and be happy because I am by your side. Just as parents delight in the laughter of their children, so I delight in hearing you laugh. I feel happy when you trust Me enough to enjoy your life.

Don't let worrying over troubles—especially things that haven't even happened yet—keep you from laughing. Live each day to its fullest by being full of My Joy. That doesn't mean you won't ever have any problems. It doesn't mean you won't ever be sad. But it *does* mean that when troubles come, you can still have Joy because the Creator of the universe is right there beside you—helping you with your problems.

So learn to laugh at your troubles . . . and you'll find that they aren't nearly so troublesome.

TALK TOGETHER

Do you believe it's possible to be joyful—even to laugh—in times of trouble or sadness? How can Jesus help you find Joy in *all* times? Can laughter make your troubles less troublesome?

LISTEN TO ME

LISTEN TO ME CONTINUALLY. I have much to communicate to you, so many people and situations in need of prayer. I am training you to set your mind on Me more and more, tuning out distractions through the help of My Spirit.

Walk with Me in holy trust, responding to My initiatives rather than trying to make things fit your plans. I died to set you free, and that includes freedom from compulsive planning. When your mind spins with a multitude of thoughts, you cannot hear My voice. A mind preoccupied with planning pays homage to the idol of control. Turn from this idolatry back to Me. Listen to Me and live abundantly!

READ TOGETHER

"My sheep listen to my voice; I know them, and they follow me."
—JOHN 10:27

READ MORE: PSALM 62:8 NKJV; JOHN 8:36; PROVERBS 19:21

Are You Listening?

Listen to Me at all times. I have so many things to tell you. There are people and situations I want you to pray for. There is help I want to give you. There are both traps and blessings I want to point out to you. Tune out all the noise of this world, and let My Spirit help you tune in to Me.

I know you have plans for this day, but check with Me first. Your plans may fit perfectly with Mine. Or I might have something even better prepared for you. Don't get so caught up in making your day go the way you have planned, that you miss out on the blessings of *My* plan. Take time to listen to Me—and I will show you how to really live!

TALK TOGETHER

What is one way to start your day listening to Jesus? How can you remember to follow Jesus all day long? What could you say to Him at night before you fall asleep?

REJOICE IN ME ALWAYS

REJOICE AND BE THANKFUL! As you walk with Me through this day, practice trusting and thanking Me all along the way. Trust is the channel through which My Peace flows into you. Thankfulness lifts you up above your circumstances.

I do My greatest works through people with grateful, trusting hearts. Rather than planning and evaluating, practice trusting and thanking Me continually. This is a paradigm shift that will revolutionize your life.

READ TOGETHER

Rejoice in the Lord always. I will say it again: Rejoice!
—PHILIPPIANS 4:4

READ MORE: PSALM 95:1–2;
PSALM 9:10; 2 CORINTHIANS 2:14 NKJV

A Joyful Heart

Rejoice! To rejoice in Me is to praise Me with joy and thankfulness. I love to hear you rejoicing. You can sing it. You can shout it. You can whisper it softly—or even pray silently. It doesn't matter *how* you do it; it matters only *that* you do it! Make this a new habit in your life.

When you rejoice in Me, I am lifted up—and I lift you up as well. Rejoicing tells Me that you know your blessings come from Me, and this makes Me want to bless you even more. I do My greatest works through people who have joyful, thankful hearts. So rejoice in Me always. In every situation. As you practice this habit of praise, your life will get better and better!

TALK TOGETHER

Sing to Jesus, "Thank you, Jesus, for loving me." Now shout a great big, "Thank you, Jesus, for loving me." Whisper, "Thank you, Jesus, for loving me." Now pray to Jesus with your joyful heart.

You Are Royalty

SIT QUIETLY IN MY PRESENCE while I bless you. Make your mind like a still pool of water, ready to receive whatever thoughts I drop into it. Rest in My sufficiency as you consider the challenges this day presents. Do not wear yourself out by worrying about whether you can cope with the pressures. Keep looking to Me and communicating with Me as we walk through this day together.

Take time to rest by the wayside, for I am not in a hurry. A leisurely pace accomplishes more than hurried striving. When you rush, you forget who you are and Whose you are. Remember that you are royalty in My kingdom.

READ TOGETHER

The Spirit himself testifies with our spirit that we are God's children. Now if we are children, then we are heirs—heirs of God and co-heirs with Christ, if indeed we share in his sufferings in order that we may also share in his glory.

—ROMANS 8:16–17

READ MORE: PSALM 37:7; 1 PETER 2:9

A Child of the King

You are a child of God. A child of the King. A member of My royal family. My own brother or sister. But does the world know it?

You are a child of God on Sunday morning, but whose are you the rest of the week? You are a child of God at church camp, but whose are you at the basketball game? You are a child of God as you lead a prayer, but whose are you when you're deciding what movie to see with your friends?

I want the world to look at you, at what you do and say, and know that you are Mine—whether it's Sunday, Tuesday morning, or Friday night.

Come to Me each morning so that I can prepare you for your day. Ask Me to help you live the day as a royal child of the King. Never forget who you are and Whose you are!

TALK TOGETHER

What does it mean to be a "child of God"? What does God's willingness to make you His child tell you about Him? How will other people know you are a child of God?

PERMEATED WITH MY PRESENCE

I AM THE CREATOR OF HEAVEN AND EARTH: Lord of all that is and all that will ever be. Although I am unimaginably vast, I choose to dwell within you, permeating you with My Presence. Only in the spirit realm could Someone so infinitely great live within someone so very small. Be awed by the Power and the Glory of My Spirit within you!

Though the Holy Spirit is infinite, *He deigns to be your Helper.* He is always ready to offer assistance; all you need to do is ask. When the path before you looks easy and straightforward, you may be tempted to *go it alone* instead of relying on Me. This is when you are in the greatest danger of stumbling. Ask My Spirit to help you as you go each step of the way. Never neglect this glorious Source of strength within you.

READ TOGETHER

"And I will pray the Father, and He will give you another Helper, that He may abide with you forever—the Spirit of truth, whom the world cannot receive, because it neither sees Him nor knows Him; but you know Him, for He dwells with you and will be in you."

—JOHN 14:16–17 NKJV

READ MORE: JOHN 16:7; ZECHARIAH 4:6

My Spirit in You

I am the Creator of heaven and earth. I am the Lord of all that is and all that will ever be. I am bigger than all the heavens. But when you choose to become one of My followers, I come to live inside you. Think about that for a moment—about who I am and how big I am. And then rejoice because My Spirit lives in you.

The Holy Spirit is always there to help you—just ask. When everything is going your way and life seems easy, you may be tempted to go it alone. But that is when you are in the greatest danger. The evil one is just waiting for you to let your guard down, to step away from My protection. Ask My Spirit to help you *every* step of the way—during hard times *and* easy times. The Spirit makes you strong.

TALK TOGETHER

Think for a moment about how big and vast and powerful God is. Now think about the truth that His Spirit lives inside His followers—inside you. How amazing is that? What power does that bring into your life?

Control Your Thoughts

Trust Me in all your thoughts. I know that some thoughts are unconscious or semiconscious, and I do not hold you responsible for those. But you can direct conscious thoughts much more than you may realize. Practice thinking in certain ways—trusting Me, thanking Me—and those thoughts become more natural. Reject negative or sinful thoughts as soon as you become aware of them. Don't try to hide them from Me; confess them and leave them with Me. Go on your way lightheartedly. This method of controlling your thoughts will keep your mind in My Presence and your feet on the *path of Peace.*

READ TOGETHER

If we confess our sins, he is faithful and just and will forgive us our sins and purify us from all unrighteousness.

—1 John 1:9

Read More: Psalm 20:7; Luke 1:79

Think the Thought

You've heard people say "Walk the walk." This means you should live the way you know is right. Well, now I am asking you to "think the thought." Think the way you know you should—with thoughts centered on Me. When you do, there is no room for thoughts of sin, revenge, hatred, self-pity, or gossip.

I know sometimes a thought just zips into your brain—you don't know where it came from and you don't want it there. Toss it right back out again. I don't hold you responsible for that kind of thought. But when you find yourself holding on to a bad thought—or returning to it over and over again like a familiar song—then you need to bring that thought to Me. Don't try to hide it. Confess it and leave it with Me. Then you can go on your way with a clear mind and a forgiven heart.

TALK TOGETHER

Think about what "walk the walk" means. Now, what do you think "think the thought" means? Are there some thoughts that you think about over and over? How can you leave them with Jesus?

Praise and Thankfulness

Let thankfulness rule in your heart. As you thank Me for blessings in your life, a marvelous thing happens. It is as if *scales fall off your eyes*, enabling you to see more and more of My glorious riches. With your eyes thus opened, you can help yourself to whatever you need from My treasure house. Each time you receive one of My golden gifts, let your thankfulness sing out praises to My Name. "Hallelujahs" are the language of heaven, and they can become the language of your heart.

A life of praise and thankfulness becomes a life filled with miracles. Instead of trying to be in control, you focus on Me and what I am doing. This is the power of praise: centering your entire being in Me. This is how I created you to live, for I made you in My own image. Enjoy abundant life by overflowing with praise and thankfulness.

READ TOGETHER

Enter his gates with thanksgiving and his courts with praise; give thanks to him and praise his name.

—Psalm 100:4

Read More: Colossians 3:15;
Acts 9:18; Revelation 19:3–6

The Language of Heaven

When you live your life praising and thanking Me for the blessings I give you each day, your life becomes filled with miracles. It is as if a blindfold has been removed from your eyes. With your eyes wide open, you see more and more of My glorious riches. So let your thankfulness sing out My praises!

A thankful heart keeps you focused on Me and what I am doing in your life. Instead of trying to be in control, you relax and make Me the Center of your life. This is the way I created you to live, and it is a way of Joy.

Your joyful praises are the language of heaven—and the true language of your heart.

TALK TOGETHER

Look to your left. Do you see a blessing? Thank God for that blessing. Now look to the right. Do you see a blessing? Thank God for that blessing. Look straight ahead. Do you see a blessing? Thank God for that blessing. Turn around and look behind you. Do you see a blessing? Thank God for that blessing.

HELP ME, JESUS!

I AM ABOVE ALL THINGS: your problems, your pain, and the swirling events in this ever-changing world. When you behold My Face, you rise above circumstances and rest with Me in *heavenly realms*. This is the way of Peace, living in the Light of My Presence. I guarantee that you will always have problems in this life, but they must not become your focus. When you feel yourself sinking in the sea of circumstances, say, *"Help me, Jesus!"* and I will draw you back to Me. If you have to say that thousands of times daily, don't be discouraged. I know your weakness, and I meet you in that very place.

READ TOGETHER

And God raised us up with Christ and seated us with him in the heavenly realms in Christ Jesus.

—EPHESIANS 2:6

READ MORE: MATTHEW 14:28–32; ISAIAH 42:3

I Will Lift You Up

I am above all things: your problems, your disappointments and hurts, and all the ever-changing events that fill up this world. And I want to lift you above all these things too.

It's a fact: You will have problems in this life. You will stumble and fall into the dirt and dust of this world. But don't give up! Don't let the dirt and dust be the only thing you see. See Me! Reach out your hand and call out, "Help me, Jesus!"

I am always near you. I will grab your hand, and I will pull you up. I will dust you off and sit you beside Me. And I will show you how—together—we can get through it all.

TALK TOGETHER

In Matthew 14, when Peter was sinking into the waves, he called out, "Lord, save me!". What does that simple prayer do? How can this prayer help you?

Truly Your Master

You cannot serve two masters. If I am truly your Master, you will desire to please Me above all others. If pleasing people is your goal, you will be enslaved to them. People can be harsh taskmasters when you give them this power over you.

If I am the Master of your life, I will also be your *First Love.* Your serving Me is rooted and grounded in My vast, unconditional Love for you. The lower you bow down before Me, the higher I lift you up into intimate relationship with Me. *The Joy of living in My Presence* outshines all other pleasures. I want you to reflect My joyous Light by living in increasing intimacy with Me.

READ TOGETHER

"No one can serve two masters. Either he will hate the one and love the other, or he will be devoted to the one and despise the other. You cannot serve both God and Money."

—Matthew 6:24

Read More: Revelation 2:4;
Ephesians 3:16–17; Psalm 16:11

Let Me Be Your Master

It is impossible to serve two masters. You will become a slave to one and then forget the other. This means that whatever you spend your time and thoughts on becomes your master. Make sure *I* am that master. Make Me your *First Love*.

If you spend too much time and energy trying to impress your friends, then friends are your master. If all you think about is trying to beat your best score, then a game is your master. If your greatest desire is getting all A's on your report card, then grades are your master.

But friends don't always know what is best for you, games can break, and school isn't forever. Only *I* am forever. Give your heart to Me and let Me be your Master. You see, I won't make you My slave—I make you My child.

TALK TOGETHER

A master is what you spend your time, energy, and thought on. What things are like masters? Who is your master? Do you have more than one? What can you do to make sure that Jesus is the one and only Master of your life?

Enjoy the Adventure

BE WILLING TO GO OUT on a limb with Me. If that is where I am leading you, it is the safest place to be. Your desire to live a risk-free life is a form of unbelief. Your longing to live close to Me is at odds with your attempts to minimize risk. You are approaching a crossroads in your journey. In order to follow Me wholeheartedly, you must relinquish your tendency to play it safe.

Let Me lead you step by step through this day. If your primary focus is on Me, you can walk along perilous paths without being afraid. Eventually, you will learn to relax and enjoy the adventure of our journey together. As long as you stay close to Me, My sovereign Presence protects you wherever you go.

READ TOGETHER

"Whoever serves me must follow me; and where I am, my servant also will be. My Father will honor the one who serves me."
—JOHN 12:26

READ MORE: PSALM 23:4; PSALM 9:10

Out on a Limb

Be willing to step out of your comfort zone. Take a risk and go out on a limb with Me. If that is where I am leading you, then out on that limb is the safest place for you to be.

You want to play it safe, avoid all the risks you can. But taking risks is part of living close to Me. Trying to live a risk-free life tells Me that you don't really trust Me. You have to make a choice: Will you keep trying to be safe at all costs? Or will you follow Me with all your heart?

I may ask you to stand up for someone who can't stand up for himself, to say no to a friend, or to tell a stranger about Me. But I'll give you the strength and the courage to do it.

Life with Me is an adventure. If you stick with Me, you'll not only have My protection, but you'll learn to relax and enjoy the adventure. So be willing to follow wherever I lead—even out on a limb.

TALK TOGETHER

Have you ever had to do something that you knew was right but wasn't much fun? When did you do something very kind or good that made you stand out from other people? Even though it was hard, did it feel good to do what you knew would make Jesus proud?

CLING TO HOPE

SOFTLY I ANNOUNCE MY PRESENCE. Shimmering hues of radiance tap gently at your consciousness, seeking entrance. Though I have all Power in heaven and on earth, I am infinitely tender with you. The weaker you are, the more gently I approach you. Let your weakness be a door to My Presence. Whenever you feel inadequate, remember that I am your *ever-present Help.*

Hope in Me, and you will be protected from depression and self-pity. Hope is like a golden cord connecting you to heaven. The more you cling to this cord, the more I bear the weight of your burdens; thus, you are lightened. Heaviness is not of My kingdom. Cling to hope, and My rays of Light will reach you through the darkness.

READ TOGETHER

God is our refuge and strength, an ever-present help in trouble.
—PSALM 46:1

READ MORE: ROMANS 12:12; ROMANS 15:13

Sometimes I Whisper

I am *always* with you. Even now, I am here with you. That soft whisper in your mind? That's from Me. That gentle tap on your heart? That's from Me too. I have all the Power in heaven and on earth. With My Might, I can control the very wind and the waves, but with you I am quiet and tender. And the more you are hurting, the more tender I am.

When others leave you feeling worthless and alone, hope in Me. My hope is not just a wish for things to be better; it is My promise to you that I will always help you. I will carry your troubles for you and lighten your heart. I am your ever-present Help, so you are never alone.

TALK TOGETHER

In Matthew 28:20, Jesus promises to be "with you always." How is He with you? How does His Presence—which never leaves you—give you hope and help?

Stay Close to Me

WORSHIP ME by living close to Me. This was My original design for man, into whom *I breathed My very breath of Life*. This is My desire for you: that you stay near Me as you walk along your life-path. Each day is an important part of that journey. Although you may feel as if you are going nowhere in this world, your spiritual journey is another matter altogether, taking you along steep, treacherous paths of adventure. That is why *walking in the Light of My Presence* is essential to keep you from stumbling. By staying close to Me, you present yourself as a *living sacrifice*. Even the most routine part of your day can be *a spiritual act of worship, holy and pleasing to Me.*

READ TOGETHER

Therefore, I urge you, brothers, in view of God's mercy, to offer your bodies as living sacrifices, holy and pleasing to God—this is your spiritual act of worship. Do not conform any longer to the pattern of this world, but be transformed by the renewing of your mind. Then you will be able to test and approve what God's will is—his good, pleasing and perfect will.

—ROMANS 12:1–2

READ MORE: GENESIS 2:7; PSALM 89:15

Your Secret Mission

Sacrifice is a difficult word to understand. And it is even more difficult to practice. It means giving up what you want for yourself in order to please or help someone else. In your relationship with Me, it means giving up control of your life—to let Me show you the way I want you to live. When you sacrifice your own will to Mine, seeking to please Me, that is worship.

I know that you want to be off on a great adventure for Me. But sometimes the greatest adventures are the ones you don't see. While your daily life may seem routine, your spiritual life can be involved in a huge, secret mission—to climb the mountain of trust and find the treasure of My Presence. When you live close to Me, you are offering yourself to Me as a living sacrifice. This pleases Me and helps Me turn your routine days into spiritual adventures of worship.

TALK TOGETHER

When did you help someone else? Or have you ever given up something you wanted in order to do something for someone else? How have your parents sacrificed for you? How has Jesus sacrificed for you?

Seek My Face

Save your best striving for seeking My Face. I am constantly communicating with you. To find Me and hear My voice, you must seek Me above all else. Anything that you desire more than Me becomes an idol. When you are determined to get your own way, you blot Me out of your consciousness. Instead of single-mindedly pursuing some goal, talk with Me about it. Let the Light of My Presence shine on this pursuit so that you can see it from My perspective. If the goal fits into My plans for you, I will help you reach it. If it is contrary to My will for you, I will gradually change the desire of your heart. *Seek Me first* and foremost; then the rest of your life will fall into place, piece by piece.

READ TOGETHER

"But seek first his kingdom and his righteousness, and all these things will be given to you as well."

—Matthew 6:33

Read More: 1 Chronicles 16:11; Proverbs 19:21 nkjv

Seek Me First

I know that you have goals—some big and some small, some just for today and some for your whole life. I want you to talk with Me about each of these goals. Don't just dive headlong into what you want to do and then ask Me to bless it. When you are determined to get your own way, you leave Me out.

Talk with Me first. Let Me help you see things from My point of view. If your goal fits My plan for your life, I will help you reach it. If it is against My plan for you, I will slowly change your heart so that you will come to want what I want. Seek Me first, and the rest of your life will fall into place, piece by piece.

TALK TOGETHER

What goals do you have—for this day, for your life? Are you leaving Jesus out of those goals? How can you put Jesus first by praying and inviting Him to show you His goals for you?

A Pattern of Good

Trust Me in every detail of your life. Nothing is random in My kingdom. *Everything that happens fits into a pattern for good, to those who love Me.* Instead of trying to analyze the intricacies of the pattern, focus your energy on trusting Me and thanking Me at all times. Nothing is wasted when you walk close to Me. Even your mistakes and sins can be recycled into something good through My transforming grace.

While you were still living in darkness, I began to shine the Light of My Presence into your sin-stained life. Finally, I *lifted you up out of the mire into My marvelous Light.* Having sacrificed My very Life for you, I can be trusted in every facet of your life.

READ TOGETHER

"But blessed is the man who trusts in the Lord, whose confidence is in him."

—Jeremiah 17:7

Read More: Romans 8:28 amp;
Psalm 40:2 amp; 1 Peter 2:9 nkjv

I Will Give You Wings

Trust Me with every detail of your life. Yes, trust Me with your life, your salvation—all the really big things. But also trust Me with your friendships, with your hopes and dreams, even with your choices about what to wear and do. Nothing is too big or too small for me. After all, I am the Creator of both Mount Everest and the tiniest grain of sand.

You are safe with Me. Bring Me your mistakes; I won't laugh at you. Bring Me your sins; I won't keep reminding you of them. I am here to forgive you, to encourage you, and to love you. Nothing is wasted when you bring everything to Me. My grace can transform even your sins and mistakes into something wonderful—much like I transform a caterpillar into a magnificent butterfly. Trust Me with everything, and I will give you "wings" to soar through your life.

TALK TOGETHER

Romans 8:28 promises that God can transform even your sins and mistakes into something good. Does that promise help you trust Him with all the details of your life? How can trusting Jesus with everything give you "wings" to soar?

Yearning for Perfection

Remember that you live in a fallen world: an abnormal world tainted by sin. Much frustration and failure result from your seeking perfection in this life. There is nothing perfect in this world except Me. That is why closeness to Me satisfies deep yearnings and fills you with Joy.

I have planted longing for perfection in every human heart. This is a good desire, which I alone can fulfill. But most people seek this fulfillment in other people and earthly pleasures or achievements. Thus they create idols, before which they bow down. *I will have no other gods before Me!* Make Me the deepest desire of your heart. Let Me fulfill your yearning for perfection.

READ TOGETHER

"You shall have no other gods before me."

—Exodus 20:3

Read More: Romans 8:22; Psalm 37:4

Seeking Perfection

I created every person—including you—with a longing for perfection. Most people try to fill this longing with things from this world. They try to have the coolest stuff and the latest fashions. They try to be the most popular in their class, or the star of the sports field or the stage. Some even try drugs or alcohol.

Some people will do anything and everything to fill that longing, except turn to Me. Whatever you desire the most—whatever you worship with your time and attention—becomes your god, your idol. But you must have no other gods before Me! Only I am God. Only I am worthy of your worship and praise. And only I can fill your longing for perfection.

TALK TOGETHER

Why does God tell us that He alone needs to be first in our lives? Why is it more important to do what God wants you to do than what you want to do? Read the 10 Commandments. Which ones tell us to put God first?

PRAY MY NAME

FIND ME in the midst of the maelstrom. Sometimes events whirl around you so quickly that they become a blur. Whisper My Name in recognition that I am still with you. Without skipping a beat in the activities that occupy you, you find strength and Peace through praying My Name. Later, when the happenings have run their course, you can talk with Me more fully.

Accept each day just as it comes to you. Do not waste your time and energy wishing for a different set of circumstances. Instead, trust Me enough to yield to My design and purposes. Remember that nothing can separate you from My loving Presence; *you are Mine.*

READ TOGETHER

Therefore God exalted him to the highest place and gave him the name that is above every name, that at the name of Jesus every knee should bow, in heaven and on earth and under the earth, and every tongue confess that Jesus Christ is Lord, to the glory of God the Father.

—PHILIPPIANS 2:9–11

READ MORE: PSALM 29:11; ISAIAH 43:1

One Word

Some days leave you feeling like Dorothy, spinning around in the middle of a tornado and terrified that you are going to fall at any moment. When that happens, whisper My Name.

Jesus.

That one simple word will help you remember that I am right beside you. One simple word declares that you *know* I am Lord of all and in control of all. One word opens your heart to My Power and Peace in the middle of the storm.

Always remember . . . I'm only one word away.

TALK TOGETHER

Think about something that is worrying you. Now close your eyes and whisper the name Jesus. Can you feel His Presence right beside you to handle those things that are too big for you to handle?

TRUE JOY

REMEMBER THAT JOY is not dependent on your circumstances. Some of the world's most miserable people are those whose circumstances seem the most enviable. People who reach the top of the ladder career-wise are often surprised to find emptiness awaiting them. True Joy is a by-product of living in My Presence. Therefore you can experience it in palaces, in prisons . . . anywhere.

Do not judge a day as devoid of Joy just because it contains difficulties. Instead, concentrate on staying in communication with Me. Many of the problems that clamor for your attention will resolve themselves. Other matters you must deal with, but I will help you with them. If you make problem solving secondary to the goal of living close to Me, you can find Joy even in your most difficult days.

READ TOGETHER

Splendor and majesty are before him; strength and joy in his dwelling place.

—1 CHRONICLES 16:27

READ MORE: HABAKKUK 3:17–19

Happiness Versus Joy

Happiness and Joy are not the same thing.

Happiness depends on this world, on what is going on around you. Happiness is when you ace the test, or make the winning shot, or you're headed for a vacation at the beach with your best friend. It depends on everything being just right. Happiness is wonderful, but it lasts only a little while.

But *Joy*—true Joy—is something entirely different. Joy doesn't depend on this world, or whether you're having a good day; it depends on *Me*. Joy is knowing that I am in control, that I love you and will take care of you—even when you flunk the test, or make the last out, or your family can't afford a vacation. Stay close to Me, and I'll give you My Joy in every situation.

TALK TOGETHER

How would you explain the difference between Joy and Happiness? Give some examples from your own life. How can depending on Jesus give you joy no matter what is happening in your life?

The Mountain Pathway

KEEP WALKING with Me along the path I have chosen for you. Your desire to live close to Me is a delight to My heart. I could instantly grant you the spiritual riches you desire, but that is not My way for you. Together we will forge a pathway up the high mountain. The journey is arduous at times, and you are weak. Someday you will dance light-footed on the high peaks; but for now your walk is often plodding and heavy. All I require of you is to take the next step, clinging to My hand for strength and direction. Though the path is difficult and the scenery dull at the moment, there are sparkling surprises just around the bend. Stay on the path I have selected for you. It is truly the *path of Life*.

READ TOGETHER

If the LORD delights in a man's way, he makes his steps firm; though he stumble, he will not fall, for the LORD upholds him with his hand.

—PSALM 37:23–24

READ MORE: ISAIAH 40:31 NKJV; PSALM 16:11 NKJV

The Journey

We are on a wonderful journey together. Though our ultimate goal is heaven, there are lots of adventures all along the way.

There are high points, such as helping a friend learn about Me. There are low points when you struggle with your own questions and doubts. There are crazy twists and turns when things in the world distract you and tempt you. Sometimes the scenery around you is beautiful—and you see Me work in amazing ways. Sometimes the scenery is frightening—like when you must stand alone for what is right. But no matter what part of the journey you are on, I am right there with you.

In good times, we leap up to the mountaintops. In difficult times, I hold your hand and keep you from falling. But at all times, I am beside you as we go along the path of Life.

TALK TOGETHER

How is your life like a journey? Have you seen high points, low points, and twists and turns? How has Jesus helped you on your journey? How does knowing that He never leaves you make you feel about the journey to come?

DELIGHT YOURSELF IN ME

SEEK TO PLEASE ME above all else. As you journey through today, there will be many choice-points along your way. Most of the day's decisions will be small ones you have to make quickly. You need some rule of thumb to help you make good choices. Many people's decisions are a combination of their habitual responses and their desire to please themselves or others. This is not My way for you. Strive to please Me in everything, not just in major decisions. This is possible only to the extent that you are living in close communion with Me. When My Presence is your deepest delight, you know almost instinctively what will please Me. A quick *glance* at Me is all you need to make the right choice. *Delight yourself in Me* more and more; seek My pleasure in all you do.

READ TOGETHER

"The one who sent me is with me; he has not left me alone, for I always do what pleases him."

—JOHN 8:29

READ MORE: HEBREWS 11:5–6; PSALM 37:4

Choices, Choices

Try to please Me *first*. Before yourself. Before others.

As you go through your day, you will have lots of choices to make. Most of them will be small, everyday choices that you have to make quickly—what to wear, who to sit with at lunch, what to do your book report on.

Many people make their choices out of habit—they choose to do the same things they always do. Or they choose things that please themselves or others. This is not what I want from you. Choose to please Me—in your big decisions and in the small ones too.

When your greatest desire is to please Me, making the right choices becomes easier. A quick, one-word prayer—*"Jesus"*—is all it takes to call upon My help and guidance. Seek to please Me in everything you do.

TALK TOGETHER

How do you make your choices—the big ones and the small ones? Do you try to please yourself, or others, or Jesus? How can you make sure you are trying to please Jesus first?

To Go on the Heights

YOU ARE FEELING WEIGHED DOWN by a plethora of problems, both big and small. They seem to require more and more of your attention, but you must not give in to those demands. When the difficulties in your life feel as if they're closing in on you, break free by spending quality time with Me. You need to remember who I AM in all My Power and Glory. Then humbly bring Me your prayers and petitions. Your problems will pale when you view them in the Light of My Presence. You can learn to *be joyful in Me, your Savior*, even in the midst of adverse circumstances. Rely on Me, *your Strength; I make your feet like the feet of a deer, enabling you to go on the heights.*

READ TOGETHER

God said to Moses, "I AM WHO I AM. This is what you are to say to the Israelites: 'I AM has sent me to you.'"

—EXODUS 3:14

READ MORE: PSALM 63:2; HABAKKUK 3:17–19

Break Away

There are times when you feel like you are drowning in problems. You feel like you just can't catch a break. There's that math problem you can't seem to figure out, that sports play you can't get right, that family problem that just gets worse and worse. It's all you can think about.

Make yourself break away from the struggles. Go outside and find a quiet place. Take a deep breath and humbly give your thoughts to Me. Remember who I AM in all My Power and Glory. I will shine the Light of My Presence on your problems. I will help you see them as they really are. And I will give you joy, in spite of your troubles. Together we can handle anything.

TALK TOGETHER

Are there troubles you need to give to Jesus in prayer? What does it mean to see your problems as Jesus sees them? How can seeing troubles through Jesus' eyes help you handle them better—even help you find Joy?

STRENGTH TO SPARE

I AM YOUR STRENGTH AND SHIELD. I plan out each day and have it ready for you long before you arise from bed. I also provide the strength you need each step of the way. Instead of assessing your energy level and wondering about what's on the road ahead, concentrate on staying in touch with Me. My Power flows freely into you through our open communication. Refuse to waste energy worrying, and you will have strength to spare.

Whenever you start to feel afraid, remember that I am your Shield. But unlike inanimate armor, I am always alert and active. My Presence watches over you continually, protecting you from both known and unknown dangers. Entrust yourself to My watchcare, which is the best security system available. *I am with you and will watch over you wherever you go.*

READ TOGETHER

The LORD is my strength and my shield; my heart trusts in him, and I am helped. My heart leaps for joy and I will give thanks to him in song.

—PSALM 28:7

READ MORE: MATTHEW 6:34; PSALM 56:3–4; GENESIS 28:15

The Best Security System Ever

I am your Strength and your Shield. Long before you get out of bed each morning, I am there, preparing and planning your day. Instead of wondering what will happen and worrying about how you will handle it, talk to Me about it. I've already got it all figured out. If you ask for My help, My Strength will flow freely into you. You will be strong enough to face whatever comes.

If you start to feel afraid, remember that I am your Shield. I'm not just a piece of cold metal—I am alive, always on the alert. I watch over you every minute, protecting you from both known and unknown dangers. I never sleep; I never take a break; I never get distracted.

Trust yourself to My Strength and My Shield—I am the best security system you'll ever find!

TALK TOGETHER

What does a shield do? How is Jesus like a shield for you? How does His being a shield give you courage and strength, as well as protection?

UNDENIABLY FREE

WALK WITH ME in the freedom of forgiveness. The path we follow together is sometimes steep and slippery. If you carry a burden of guilt on your back, you are more likely to stumble and fall. At your request, I will remove the heavy load from you and bury it at the foot of the cross. When I unburden you, you are undeniably free! Stand up straight and tall in My Presence so that no one can place more burdens on your back. Look into My Face and feel the warmth of My Love-Light shining upon you. It is this unconditional Love that frees you from both fears and sins. Spend time basking in the Light of My Presence. As you come to know Me more and more intimately, you grow increasingly free.

READ TOGETHER

Praise be to the Lord, to God our Savior, who daily bears our burdens.

—PSALM 68:19

READ MORE: 1 JOHN 1:7–9; 1 JOHN 4:18

Be Free

I see you carrying around a bunch of burdens: guilt over something you said to your mom or dad, anger at a friend's betrayal, sadness at a disappointment. I did not create you to walk around with such heavy loads. They pull you down and make you stumble.

When you are carrying so much weight, you are much more likely to fall. When you are hauling around guilt and anger, you are much more likely to sin by doing or saying something you shouldn't.

I want you to give your burdens to Me. Just hand them over and don't look back. That's why I died on the cross—to free you from your burdens. Let Me sweep them away with My forgiveness. Let Me set you free!

TALK TOGETHER

How can feelings like anger, guilt, and sadness be like burdens? Can you trust Jesus to lift away your burdens? Are there burdens you need to give to Jesus?

DESIGNED TO NEED ME

YOUR NEEDS AND MY RICHES are a perfect fit. I never meant for you to be self-sufficient. Instead, I designed you to need Me not only for daily bread but also for fulfillment of deep yearnings. I carefully crafted your longings and feelings of incompleteness to point you to Me. Therefore, do not try to bury or deny these feelings. Beware also of trying to pacify these longings with lesser gods: people, possessions, power.

Come to Me in all your neediness, with defenses down and with desire to be blessed. As you spend time in My Presence, your deepest longings are fulfilled. Rejoice in your neediness, which enables you to find intimate completion in Me.

READ TOGETHER

My purpose is that they may be encouraged in heart and united in love, so that they may have the full riches of complete understanding, in order that they may know the mystery of God, namely, Christ, in whom are hidden all the treasures of wisdom and knowledge.

—COLOSSIANS 2:2–3

READ MORE: PHILIPPIANS 4:19; PSALM 84:11–12 NKJV

Be Glad You Are Needy

Your needs and My riches are a perfect fit—like the pieces of a puzzle that join together to make a beautiful picture.

I never meant for you to "go it alone," to do it all by yourself. I designed you to need Me, not only for your daily bread but also to fill that deep emptiness inside you. I created that emptiness to lead you to Me. It's part of My plan. So don't try to pretend the emptiness doesn't exist. And don't try to fill it with the lesser gods of this world: people, possessions, and power.

Come to Me with all your needs. Let your defenses down and seek My blessings. As you spend time with Me, your emptiness gets filled with My Love, Joy, and Peace. Be glad you are needy—that helps you get filled up with Me.

TALK TOGETHER

In what ways do you need Jesus every day? Name five ways Jesus has been there for you in the past. Name five ways that you need Jesus today and in the future.

SAFE AND SECURE

I WANT YOU TO KNOW how safe and secure you are in My Presence. That is a fact, totally independent of your feelings. You are on your way to heaven; nothing can prevent you from reaching that destination. There you will see Me face to Face, and your Joy will be off the charts by any earthly standards. Even now, you are never separated from Me, though you must see Me through eyes of faith. I will walk with you till the end of time and onward into eternity.

Although My Presence is a guaranteed promise, that does not necessarily change your feelings. When you forget I am with you, you may experience loneliness or fear. It is through awareness of My Presence that Peace displaces negative feelings. Practice the discipline of walking consciously with Me through each day.

READ TOGETHER

The LORD gives strength to his people; the LORD blesses his people with peace.

—PSALM 29:11

READ MORE: JOHN 10:28–29; 1 CORINTHIANS 13:12

You Are Safe with Me

You are completely safe and secure in My Presence—even when you don't feel that way. You are never separated from Me because I never leave you.

When you forget that I am with you, you may feel lonely or afraid. If that happens, say a prayer or whisper My Name: "Jesus." This will remind you that I am still right beside you. As you focus on Me, I will replace your loneliness and fear with My Peace.

As wonderful as My Peace is now, it is nothing compared to heaven. In heaven I will still be right by your side, but you will be able to *see* Me. You and I will talk face-to-Face. And your Joy will be bigger and better than anything you can imagine!

TALK TOGETHER

Do you ever forget that Jesus is with you? When does that happen? What can you do to remind yourself that Jesus is always right there with you? What do you imagine it will be like to see Jesus face to Face?

Peace in Your Heart

I HAVE PROMISED *to meet all your needs according to My glorious riches.* Your deepest, most constant need is for My Peace. I have planted Peace in the garden of your heart, where I live, but there are weeds growing there too: pride, worry, selfishness, unbelief. I am the Gardener, and I am working to rid your heart of those weeds. I do My work in various ways. When you sit quietly with Me, I shine the Light of My Presence directly into your heart. In this heavenly Light, Peace grows abundantly and weeds shrivel up. I also send trials into your life. When you trust Me in the midst of trouble, Peace flourishes and weeds die away. Thank Me for troublesome situations; the Peace they can produce *far outweighs* the trials you endure.

READ TOGETHER

For our light and momentary troubles are achieving for us an eternal glory that far outweighs them all.

—2 CORINTHIANS 4:17

READ MORE: PHILIPPIANS 4:19; 2 THESSALONIANS 3:16 NKJV

Getting Rid of the Weeds

I promise to meet all your needs. And while you may not realize it, your greatest need is for My Peace.

I am the Gardener of your heart, planting seeds of peace. But the world also tosses in seeds. These seeds grow into weeds of pride, worry, and selfishness. If these weeds aren't ripped out quickly, they will choke out all your peace.

I get rid of those weeds in different ways. Sometimes, when you sit quietly in prayer, My Light shines on the weeds and they shrivel up. But other times, I use troubles to encourage you to trust Me. And that trust kills the weeds.

So thank Me for troubles, as well as joys. Because I use them both to make your heart My garden of Peace.

TALK TOGETHER

How is Jesus like a gardener for your heart? Are there weeds of pride, worry, selfishness, or doubt in your life? How do you tear out those weeds? What would happen if you let the Light of Jesus shine on them?

Thankfulness

THANK ME for the very things that are troubling you. You are on the brink of rebellion, precariously close to shaking your fist in My Face. You are tempted to indulge in just a little complaining about My treatment of you. But once you step over that line, torrents of rage and self-pity can sweep you away. The best protection against this indulgence is thanksgiving. It is impossible to thank Me and curse Me at the same time.

Thanking Me for trials will feel awkward and contrived at first. But if you persist, your thankful words, prayed in faith, will eventually make a difference in your heart. Thankfulness awakens you to My Presence, which overshadows all your problems.

READ TOGETHER

Rejoice in the Lord always. I will say it again: Rejoice! Let your gentleness be evident to all. The Lord is near. Do not be anxious about anything, but in everything, by prayer and petition, with thanksgiving, present your requests to God.

—PHILIPPIANS 4:4–6

READ MORE: PSALM 116:17 NKJV; PSALM 100:2 NKJV

Your Best Protection

I am always near. So I know that sometimes you get angry at Me—and may even feel like shaking your fist in My Face. You are tempted to complain about the way I am treating you. You want to rebel against Me. But that is a dangerous thing to do. Once you step over that line, rivers of rage and self-pity can sweep you away.

Your best protection is to thank Me for the things that are troubling you. You see, it is impossible for you to thank Me and complain at the same time. It may feel weird at first to thank Me when you are upset with Me. But keep trying. Your thankful words, prayed in faith, will change your heart and bring you closer to Me.

TALK TOGETHER

Have you ever been upset with Jesus? How can thanking Him even when things are not going like you want change your heart? Thank Jesus right now, no matter how you feel. In this prayer, don't ask for anything. Don't complain. Just thank Him.

RELY ON ME ALONE

LET ME HELP YOU through this day. The challenges you face are far too great for you to handle alone. You are keenly aware of your helplessness in the scheme of events you face. This awareness opens up a choice: to doggedly go it alone or to walk with Me in humble steps of dependence. Actually, this choice is continually before you, but difficulties highlight the decision-making process. So *consider it all joy whenever you are enveloped in various trials.* These are gifts from Me, reminding you to rely on Me alone.

READ TOGETHER

Because you are my help, I sing in the shadow of your wings. My soul clings to you; your right hand upholds me.

—PSALM 63:7–8

READ MORE: PSALM 46:1; JAMES 1:2–3 AMP

Don't Go It Alone

It is a simple fact: You cannot make it by yourself. More importantly, you don't *have* to make it by yourself. It's up to you.

Yes, there will be days when everything goes just the way you planned. You've got everything under control, and you are living on top of the world. But then—BAM! Trouble—*big* trouble—comes and yanks away the control you thought you had. An illness, an accident, it's something you never saw coming.

You know you need help. Let Me help you. I already know the answers. Let Me guide you to them. But first you have to choose: Do you stubbornly go it alone? Or do you humbly come to Me and let Me help you? Please, choose Me.

TALK TOGETHER

Have you ever been afraid, or sad, or lonely? Then someone you loved reached out and held your hand. Suddenly, you didn't feel as bad. Reach out your hand and let Jesus overcome your troubles, sadness, anger, and loneliness.

BUILD YOUR HOUSE ON THE ROCK

I SPEAK TO YOU from deepest heaven. You hear Me in the depths of your being. *Deep calls unto deep.* You are blessed to hear Me so directly. Never take this privilege for granted. The best response is a heart overflowing with gratitude. I am training you to cultivate a thankful mind-set. This is like *building your house on a firm rock, where life's storms cannot shake you.* As you learn these lessons, you are to teach them to others. I will open up the way before you, one step at a time.

READ TOGETHER

"Therefore everyone who hears these words of mine and puts them into practice is like a wise man who built his house on the rock. The rain came down, the streams rose, and the winds blew and beat against that house; yet it did not fall, because it had its foundation on the rock."

—MATTHEW 7:24–25

READ MORE: PSALM 42:7–8 NKJV; PSALM 95:1–2

Rock or Sand?

The wise man who builds his house on the rock is able to get safely through the storms. And the foolish man who builds his house on the sand—well, his house goes *splat!*

But sometimes in this world, it can be tough to figure out what is rock and what is sand. The world tells you first one thing and then another. Sometimes your teachers say one thing and your parents say another. How can you know what is rock and what is sand?

I am the Rock. Come to Me in prayer, and I will show you what is true, what can be trusted, what is real. Ask My Spirit to guide you as you study My Word. Anything that does not agree with My Word is sand and should not be trusted. Build your house upon the Rock of My Word. And then trust that I will help you stand firm when the storms come—because I will.

TALK TOGETHER

In Matthew 7, Jesus tells the story of building on the rock and on the sand. In this parable, what is the sand? What is the rock? How can you build your life on the Rock of Jesus?

UNPLUG

LIE DOWN IN GREEN PASTURES of Peace. Learn to unwind whenever possible, resting in the Presence of your Shepherd. This electronic age keeps My children "wired" much of the time, too tense to find Me in the midst of their moments. I built into your very being the need for rest. How twisted the world has become when people feel guilty about meeting this basic need! How much time and energy they waste by being always on the go rather than taking time to seek My direction for their lives.

I have called you to walk with Me down *paths of Peace*. I want you to blaze a trail for others who desire to live in My peaceful Presence. I have chosen you less for your strengths than for your weaknesses, which amplify your need for Me. Depend on Me more and more, and I will shower Peace on all your paths.

READ TOGETHER

By the seventh day God had finished the work he had been doing; so on the seventh day he rested from all his work. And God blessed the seventh day and made it holy, because on it he rested from all the work of creating that he had done.

—GENESIS 2:2–3

READ MORE: PSALM 23:1–3; LUKE 1:79

Wired

Television, cell phones, the Internet—this electronic age keeps you "wired" much of the time. When you're an electrical appliance, being wired is a good thing. But when you are human, being wired can be exhausting. It also makes it harder for you to find Me in your moments.

I created you to need rest. At creation, I even gave you the example of rest by taking a break from all My work. But the world has gotten so twisted that it makes you feel guilty about taking time to rest. This is a trick of the devil. If he can keep you "wired" most of the time—too busy to even stop and look for Me—then he wins.

Tell the devil to get lost. Then lie down, close your eyes, and whisper, "Jesus, help me rest." I'll cover you with a blanket of Peace and watch over you as you rest in Me.

TALK TOGETHER

How much time each day do you spend "wired"? Do you ever think that you need time to just rest? What can you do to make time to unplug and find rest in Jesus?

Live in My Love

Seek to live in My Love, which *covers a multitude of sins*: both yours and others'. Wear My Love like a cloak of Light, covering you from head to toe. Have no fear, for *perfect Love decimates fear.* Look at other people through lenses of Love; see them from My perspective. This is how you walk in the Light, and it pleases Me.

I want My body of believers to be radiant with the Light of My Presence. How I grieve when pockets of darkness increasingly dim the Love-Light. Return to Me, your *First Love!* Gaze at Me in the splendor of holiness, and My Love will once again envelop you in Light.

READ TOGETHER

Above all, love each other deeply, because love covers over a multitude of sins.

—1 Peter 4:8

Read More: 1 John 4:18; Revelation 2:4

Love Takes Care of It All

Love is the key to My kingdom. Above all else, I want you to love Me with all your heart, mind, body, and soul. When that happens, you open yourself up to receive My Love for you. And My Love changes everything.

My Love *covers over a multitude of sins*—both your sins and the sins of others. This means that once you bring your sins to Me, they are forgiven and completely forgotten. It also means that you will be able to forgive others, because you will see them through the eyes of My Love. You'll be able to look beyond a bully's hateful words, for example, and see someone who feels bad about himself. When someone lies, you will see more than just the lies: You'll see a person who is afraid to tell the truth.

Choose to see others through the eyes of My Love. And My Love will take care of it all.

TALK TOGETHER

How can love cover over "a multitude of sins"? If you were to look at people through the eyes of Jesus' love, how would that change the way you see them? Would it help you forgive those who have hurt you?

FOCUS ON ME

MAKE ME YOUR FOCAL POINT as you move through this day. Just as a spinning ballerina must keep returning her eyes to a given point to maintain her balance, so you must keep returning your focus to Me. Circumstances are in flux, and the world seems to be whirling around you. The only way to keep your balance is to *fix your eyes on Me*, the One who never changes. If you gaze too long at your circumstances, you will become dizzy and confused. Look to Me, refreshing yourself in My Presence, and your steps will be steady and sure.

READ TOGETHER

Let us fix our eyes on Jesus, the author and perfecter of our faith, who for the joy set before him endured the cross, scorning its shame, and sat down at the right hand of the throne of God.

—HEBREWS 12:2

READ MORE: PSALM 102:27; 1 JOHN 3:19–20

In the Right Direction

When you learn to ride a bike, you quickly learn to keep your eyes on where you want the bike to go. If you look away, then you're likely to go off in the wrong direction—and crash into a ditch or a tree! Wherever your eyes go, your bike soon follows.

Your thoughts are much the same. Keep your thoughts focused on Me and My will for you. People and situations change all the time. And the world whirls around like the scenery flying past a car window. If you focus too long on the world, you will get dizzy and confused. But I never change. Keep your thoughts on Me, and I will keep you moving in the right direction.

TALK TOGETHER

What happens when you let the world become the focus of your thoughts? Is it confusing? How can you focus your thoughts on Jesus instead? When you choose to focus on Jesus instead of the world, how does your life change?

REFLECT MY LIGHT

I AM THE LIGHT OF THE WORLD. People crawl through their lives cursing the darkness, but all the while I am shining brightly. I desire each of My followers to be a Light-bearer. The Holy Spirit who lives in you can shine from your face, making Me visible to people around you. Ask My Spirit to live through you as you wend your way through this day. Hold My hand in joyful trust, for I never leave your side. The Light of My Presence is shining upon you. Brighten up the world by reflecting who I AM.

READ TOGETHER

"You are the light of the world. A city on a hill cannot be hidden. Neither do people light a lamp and put it under a bowl. Instead they put it on its stand, and it gives light to everyone in the house. In the same way, let your light shine before men, that they may see your good deeds and praise your Father in heaven."

—MATTHEW 5:14–16

READ MORE: JOHN 8:12; 2 CORINTHIANS 3:18; EXODUS 3:14

Be a Light

This world is full of darkness. But I am the Light of the World. When you choose to follow Me, the Holy Spirit who lives inside you can shine out from your face. Take My Light and carry it into the world around you.

Be My hands by helping others, and love them with My Love. Ask My Spirit to live through you as you make your way through this day. Hold My hand with joy in your heart—trusting that I never leave your side. The Light of My Presence is shining on you. Brighten up the world around you by reflecting this Light—showing *Me* to others.

TALK TOGETHER

In what ways is Jesus the Light of the World? Of your life? How does He shine both *on* you and *in* you? In what ways can you reflect His Light and share it with the world?

If you enjoyed this book, you may be interested in these other books from the author of *Jesus Calling*®

Peace in His Presence
quotes with inspirational images
ISBN 9780718034160

Jesus Calling 365 Devotions for Kids
adapted for children 8–12
ISBN 9781400316342

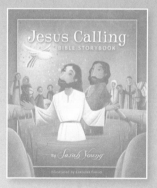

Jesus Calling Bible Storybook
Bible stories and devotions
ISBN 9781400320332

Learn more at JesusCalling.com